# RURAL
# POVERTY

# RURAL POVERTY

## Special Causes
## and Policy Reforms

Edited by
HARRELL R. RODGERS, JR.,
and GREGORY WEIHER

*Prepared under the auspices
of the Policy Studies Organization*

Studies in Social Welfare Policies and Programs, Number 12
Stuart S. Nagel, Series Editor

GREENWOOD PRESS
NEW YORK • WESTPORT, CONNECTICUT • LONDON

**Library of Congress Cataloging-in-Publication Data**

Rural poverty.

(Studies in social welfare policies and programs,
ISSN 8755-5360 ; no. 12)
Bibliography: p.
Includes index.
1. Social service, Rural—United States. 2. United
States—Rural conditions. Rural poor—United States—
Social conditions. I. Rodgers, Harrell R. II. Weiher,
Gregory. III. Series.
HV91.R772 1989 362.5 '8 '0973 88-35817
ISBN 0-313-26630-1 (lib. bdg. : alk. paper)

British Library Cataloguing in Publication Data is available.

Library of Congress Catalog Card Number: 88-35817
ISBN: 0-313-26630-1
ISSN: 8755-5360

First published in 1989

Greenwood Press, Inc.
88 Post Road West, Westport, Connecticut 06881

Printed in the United States of America

The paper used in this book complies with the
Permanent Paper Standard issued by the National
Information Standards Organization (Z39.48-1984).

10 9 8 7 6 5 4 3 2 1

**Copyright Acknowledgement**

The editors and publisher are grateful to the following for granting the
use of their material:

Leif Jensen, "Rural-Urban Differences in the Utilization and
Ameliorative Effects of Welfare Programs," *Policy Studies Review*
7, no. 4 (Summer 1988): 728-94.

# Contents

# *Illustrations*

**FIGURES**

**TABLES**

# Acknowledgments

This research was made possible by a Ford Foundation grant, a Henry J. Leir Foundation grant, and a number of university grants to individual authors. We would like to express our appreciation for their help in allowing us to fill some of the void in the research on rural poverty. We would also like to extend our thanks to Professor Stuart S. Nagel, the guiding light of the Policy Studies Organization, for suggesting the topic and for writing the grant proposals that financed much of the work.

# *Introduction*

## HARRELL R. RODGERS, JR.,
## and GREGORY WEIHER

The preponderance of research on American poverty has an urban bias. Indeed, rural poverty receives scant attention compared to the highly visible poverty of urban America. This volume seeks to improve insights into rural poverty by addressing two questions: (1) do rural and urban poverty result from different causes? and (2) are special programs needed to ameliorate rural poverty? The chapters here document that the answer to both questions is yes. Poverty in rural and urban areas is often caused by many of the same factors, but there are important differences. The studies here conclude that rural poverty is more likely than urban poverty to be caused by inadequate employment compensation, rising unemployment, depression in the agricultural sector, and welfare eligibility rules that exclude significant proportions of the deserving poor. The rural poor also differ from the urban poor in some significant ways. The rural poor are more likely to be employed, more apt to be members of married-couple families, less likely to be children, less likely to be minority, more liable to have assets but a negative income. The chapters document and examine the reasons why welfare programs are unresponsive to the causal and demographic differences between rural and urban poverty, and suggest alternative reforms to mitigate rural poverty.

## POVERTY RATES IN RURAL AMERICA

One indication of the design flaws of extant welfare programs is that, by conventional measures, poverty rates are higher in rural than in urban regions of the United States. Yet, the rural poor are much less likely to receive assistance. One reason is that the rural poor are more often employed and are more likely to have assets that make them benefit ineligible. As several of the authors point out, it is widely believed that the rural poor are less needy because they may have some assets. This volume begins with a study that addresses this point. Donald Lerman and James Mikesell examine the changes in the distribution of poverty in rural and urban areas that would result from modifying the conventional poverty measure to include the annuity value of household net worth. Their study, "Rural and Urban Poverty: An Income/Net Worth Approach," is based on data drawn from the 1983 Survey of Consumer Finances, a household level data base containing detailed income, wealth, and demographic information.

Use of an income/wealth measure does produce some important shifts in the location and demography of the poverty population. Still, using either the income or income/net worth measure revealed that poverty was higher in rural areas (21.1 percent) than in the United States as a whole (15.6 percent) or in all urban areas (14.7 percent). Breaking urban America into five categories revealed that rural poverty rates were above those of some urban areas and below those of others. The central cities displayed the most severe poverty; the suburbs had the lowest rates. The federal government's income standard yields poverty rates 4.4 times the suburban rate. The income/net worth measure showed central city poverty to be six times the suburban level. By both measures, the second and third highest poverty rates were in rural areas and central cities of under 2 million population. In terms of demographic characteristics, those more often found to be in poverty under the income/net worth measure were young, renter, and large central city resident households.

Poverty rates, therefore, remain very high in both central city and rural areas even when the annuity value of net worth is taken into consideration.

## UTILIZATION OF WELFARE PROGRAMS

In "Rural-Urban Differences in the Utilization and Ameliorative Effects of Welfare Programs," Leif Jensen documents the discriminatory impact of welfare programs. Jensen's analysis reveals that, despite comparatively high poverty rates in nonmetropolitan areas, the rural poor were much less likely than their urban counterparts to receive welfare. Moreover, rural welfare recipients received considerably less welfare income, on average, than metropolitan recipients. Accordingly, the ameliorative effect of welfare was lowest in rural areas and highest in central cities. Logistic regression analysis revealed that rural poor families were less likely to receive welfare than those in metropolitan areas because they were more likely to be working, older, childless, and headed by a married couple.

Jensen's findings document a substantial bias of current welfare programs toward the needs of the urban poor. His findings also reveal some of the limitations of current welfare reform efforts. The major welfare reform legislation passed by Congress in 1988 (the Family Welfare Reform Act) stresses remedial training and job placement services. While some provisions of the act would be beneficial to the rural poor, the package of reforms would be considerably more beneficial to the urban than the rural poor.

## LABOR FORCE PARTICIPATON

There are, however, policy approaches that would have beneficial impacts on subgroups of the poor, regardless of geographic location. In "Labor Force Participation and Poverty Status among Rural and Urban Women Who Head Families," Eleanor Cautley and Doris Slesinger examine differentials in the propensity to be living in poverty among women who head families with minor children. Four groups of mothers are examined: residents of central cities, suburbs, small towns, and rural areas. After controlling for the effects of the mother's race, marital status, education, work status, and ages of her children, single mothers in central cities and small towns are found to have the highest rates of poverty (48 percent and 45 percent respectively) followed closely by those in rural areas (41 percent). Suburban single mothers are least likely to live in poverty (33 percent).

The data analysis reveals that employment status is the strongest predictor of poverty, followed by education and marital status. A subanalysis of women who work full time reveals major differences in earned income, with suburban women earning the highest incomes, followed by women living in central cities, then rural areas, and finally small towns. A decomposition of this difference reveals that about two-thirds of the variance is due to pay scales, and only one-third is due to the structure of occupational opportunity.

One conclusion of Cautley and Slesinger is that raising the minimum wage would do more to help poor working mothers than increasing welfare benefits. They also recommend improved child care, better access to education and training programs, increased enforcement of child care awards, and increased pay equity between men and women.

## THE IMPACT OF THE FARM CRISIS

In "Impacts of the Farm Financial Crisis of the 1980s on Resources and Poverty in Agriculturally Dependent Counties in the United States," Steve

Murdock et al. provide an in-depth examination of the impact of the farm financial crisis of the 1980s on agriculturally dependent areas in the United States. Their analysis reveals that the crisis has resulted in a larger proportion of producers leaving agriculture than at any other period since the 1930s, and in a substantial decline in agricultural trade centers, particularly in the Midwest and Great Plains states. Although the crisis has obviously had clear and widely known effects on the income of producers, its impacts on overall levels of income and rates of poverty in rural areas has not been adequately analyzed.

Using a classification of counties based on criteria similar to those utilized by L. D. Bender et al. (1985), 472 agriculturally dependent counties are identified in the United States. Parameters derived from U.S. Department of Agriculture data and from extensive surveys of producers, business operators, and employees in rural communities conducted by the authors are then used to simulate the likely impacts of different levels of farm failure on aggregate and household income levels in agriculturally dependent counties. Specifically, the effects on the incomes of producers' households and on the households of business operators and employees in rural communities are examined.

The results show substantial income effects. Many producer households, particularly under assumptions that income is spent for debt retirement rather than for household living expenses, can be expected to experience a significant reduction in income, and many could be forced to live at poverty levels. Similar patterns are evident for business operators and employees in rural communities in such counties. Among many employees marginal income levels are accentuated by the crisis, leading to a substantial increase in the rates of poverty among this group.

Murdock et al. continue with a discussion of the likely long-term implications of the farm crisis, and the consequences of failing to address the effects of the crisis, on producers and rural community residents. It is suggested that the crisis is a rural not just a farm crisis and that, if left unaddressed, the crisis could result in a long-term loss of economic opportunities and accentuated rates of poverty in agriculturally dependent counties in the United States.

## ALTERING REFORM APPROACHES

David Debertin and Craig Infanger augment this analysis by examining the differential causes and cures for poverty in rural areas. In "Rural Poverty, Welfare Eligibility Farm Programs, and the Negative Income Tax," Debertin and Infanger develop four paradigms that depict the causes of poverty for rural farm and rural nonfarm residents. They conclude that rural poverty in low-income regions where a subsistence agriculture dominates is caused primarily by deficiencies in human and physical capital.

Rural poverty occurring as a result of the farm financial crisis of the 1980s is caused by a different set of factors, many of which affect the general farm economy and are outside the control of the individual farmer.

Depending on the cause, Debertin and Infanger point out, strategies and policy options for alleviating rural poverty must vary. A major problem to be contended with is that most of the rural farm poor do not qualify for welfare programs. They are disqualified because they often have a positive net worth, even when they have very low, even negative, incomes. Neither do they receive much assistance from commodity price supports and other farm programs because these programs are designed to assist larger, more productive farms. The trap for these rural poor, Debertin and Infanger contend, is that welfare programs are designed with the urban poor in mind, just as farm assistance programs are designed to aid successful farmers.

To aid the rural poor, they argue, the government's approach to rural poverty needs to be rethought. One option would be for the government to provide job training and financial assistance to farmers exiting agriculture. This approach could be designed around the strategies discussed by Robert Plotnick in Chapter 6. Another option would be for the government to alter the asset standard for welfare eligibility for low-income farmers. A more comprehensive welfare approach would be a negative income tax, designed to give the rural poor an economic base and an incentive to earn above that base.

Plotnick takes a more unique approach to helping the rural poor. In "Can Income Transfers Promote Economic Development in Poor, Rural Communities?" Plotnick addresses the question of whether government transfer payments (e.g., Aid to Families with Dependent Children [AFDC], food stamps, Medicare, and Social Security) can contribute to economic development and job creation in small, rural communities. Plotnick's interest is whether income transfers can be combined with other economic strategies to serve the dual purpose of "safety net" and economic development tool. The attractiveness of the plan is that if the states can design such strategies, they would have no net increase in social welfare costs. If the approach succeeded, it would lower state benefit expenditures.

Plotnick examines the potential of three types of transfer programs: retirement programs, unemployment compensation, and welfare benefits. The retirement programs (Social Security, Medicare, railroad retirement, military pensions, and state and local benefits) have the advantage of not requiring the recipient to live in a specific community. Retirees can relocate to rural areas, bringing their purchasing power and investments. The result is the equivalent of a basic industry. Plotnick examines the implications of such a strategy and the type of rural communities most likely to employ it successfully.

Plotnick's second focus is the innovative use of unemployment insurance (UI) payments to stimulate rural economies. He examines the likely implications for rural communities of using UI funds to retrain displaced workers, provide job search assistance, and promote self-employment and relocation. Plotnick concludes that the potential of using UI to promote self-employment, especially if some lessons from similar programs in Europe are incorporated, is at least promising.

Plotnick also reviews the literature on the impact of welfare benefits on rural development. He concludes that only under limited circumstances can the impact be beneficial.

In "Rural Economic Development Policies for the Midwestern States," Stanley Johnson et al. take a more comprehensive approach to rural development. The authors explore different perceptions of rural economic development and discuss how they relate to the economic base and economic performance of communities. Focusing on the Midwest, they also evaluate the various policy recommendations designed to deal with economic problems of rural areas.

The rural poverty conditions in the Midwest differ from other regions in that relatively high levels of infrastructure and human capital are present and the region has already enjoyed periods of relative prosperity. These conditions create a unique rural poverty situation. Demographic and economic performance data are utilized to characterize the rural sector of the Midwest and to contrast its performance with urban areas.

As the authors point out, perspectives on economic development differ and each has disparate policy implications. Perspectives on rural economic development held by state and local policymakers include (a) restoring a region to a previous level of economic performance and social well-being, (b) addressing economic inequities of a region, and (c) dealing with the under-performance of a region in relation to its potential and its resource base.

Policy intiatives for addressing rural economic development include (a) increasing resources, (b) expanding markets, (c) developing new technologies, (d) developing new institutions, and (e) capturing benefits of agglomeration economics. The authors discuss the policy implications resulting from each of these strategies.

The authors note that these varied approaches to the economic development problem suggest a lack of consensus on a rural development policy. An alternative is a framework to monitor economic performance and to evaluate policy actions. The last section of the chapter proposes a framework and a process to provide this monitoring and evaluation information, and it discusses issues and problems in the design and implementation of rural economic development in this framework.

## CONCLUSIONS

Clearly, much of the rural poverty in America results from causes different from those that cause urban poverty, and it can be ameliorated only by programs designed to deal with the particular problems and needs of rural citizens and rural economic systems. This is not to say that the rural poor are not helped by extant welfare programs or that some of the reforms currently being debated by Congress would not be beneficial to the rural poor. In fact, the provisions of the Family Welfare Reform Act that provide incentives to the states to raise AFDC benefits, require all states to extend benefits to two-parent families, and liberalize work-related deductions will be quite helpful to the rural poor. Child care, child support, and health care bills currently being debated by Congress would also extend much needed benefits to the rural poor. Still, asset limits that might be reasonable for the urban poor unfairly exclude a significant proportion of the deserving rural poor, especially those caught in the farm crisis.

The rural poor would also benefit from an increase in the minimum wage, retraining, job placement, and small-business start-up programs for those exiting the farm economy, and farm-support programs directed more toward the small farmer. Most important, however, rural economies frequently need restructuring and stimulation. This is often the most creative solution and the greatest challenge.

# 1

# *Rural and Urban Poverty:*
# *An Income/Net Worth Approach*

## DONALD L. LERMAN and JAMES J. MIKESELL

## INTRODUCTION

Interest in the locational distribution of the poverty population dates at least to the beginnings of the War on Poverty in the mid-1960s. Burton Weisbrod then argued that where the poor are located is of fundamental importance in forming antipoverty strategies. High concentrations of poverty in rural or urban areas or in certain geographic regions may call for different policies than would an even distribution of the nation's poor. Public antipoverty efforts must take account of significant rural/urban and regional differences in the number and demographic makeup of those in poverty. For example, the effectiveness of a public employment program may depend on whether the poor in an area are largely young and employable or elderly and in poor health. The effectiveness of policies to train the unskilled, to invest in local infrastructure, to increase benefits to single-parent households, or to reach out to specific groups, such as the elderly, minorities, or eligible nonparticipants in government programs, may also vary widely by region and by rural/urban location.

How poverty is defined is also of significance in recognizing and analyzing economic disadvantage by location. While the official poverty definition is based on a household's current income and composition, other factors may significantly affect the level of need or economic deprivation a household experiences. Literacy, health, housing situation, and level of household wealth clearly affect the economic position of a household. Many economically depressed areas, which are often rural, have historically fared poorly in such nonincome factors. Thus, a conventional income-based analysis of regional variation in poverty rates will be incomplete, and it may well understate true regional differences in economic need.

Household wealth, which represents the stock of household real and financial resources whereas income represents the financial flow, is perhaps the most natural of the nonincome factors to be included in a poverty measure. With approximately two-thirds of all households owning their own home and with high housing inflation in the late 1970s generally increasing the significance of home ownership in a typical household's well-being, household wealth constitutes a large and growing proportion of total household resources. The use of mortgage and nonmortgage household debt has also increased in recent years and can markedly affect household net worth. Unlike other nonincome factors, such as literacy or health status, nonhuman wealth is directly expressed in dollar terms and can be readily converted to an income flow.

Omitting wealth (net worth) from the official income-based poverty measure would be less important if wealth and income were perfectly or very closely correlated, for then income would be a good proxy for both factors. However, the correlation between net worth and income is only about 0.5, and much of that is directly attributable to income from assets.[1] Since there are rural/urban and regional differences between wealth and income distributions, a combined income and wealth measure of economic well-being may yield a significantly different profile of persons in poverty. Income and wealth distributions also vary systematically with age, tenure, and other family characteristics. Thus, rural/urban and regional differences in these factors can result in widely different effects of including wealth in measuring family resources.

More concretely, a rural resident is currently one-third more likely than an urban resident to be in poverty by the conventional income-based measure. (Official 1983 census poverty rates were 18.3 percent in nonmetropolitan areas and 13.8 percent in metropolitan areas [Bentley 1987]). Elderly households, who tend to have low incomes but higher than average wealth, constitute a greater proportion of the rural population. Therefore, including wealth in measuring poverty may narrow the rural/urban gap in poverty. Additionally, higher wealth is associated with home ownership, self-employment, and farm residence, factors more prevalent in rural areas. On the other hand, median wealth is lower in rural areas than in urban areas according to 1983 data (Lerman 1988). Thus, with potentially offsetting effects, it is not clear how accounting for wealth would affect the locational distribution of poverty.

This chapter analyzes the impact of a modified poverty measure that considers net worth on the distribution of U.S. poverty, particularly between rural and urban areas. Our combined income/wealth measure of poverty is the sum of current income and the annual annuity value of net worth. Estimating poverty under both the conventional income and income/wealth measures, we examine the number and characteristics of the rural and urban poor. The 1983 Survey of Consumer Finances (SCF) provided household level data with detailed income, wealth, and demographic information. Questions we address include: What is the size and composition of the rural and urban poverty populations? How does the modified poverty definition alter the distribution of the rural and urban poor by age, sex, race, marital status, education, tenure, occupation, and other selected characteristics? How many of the rural and urban poor, as currently measured, would still be considered poor under the alternative income/wealth measure?

## MEASURING POVERTY

Prior to the mid-1960s, poverty for U.S. families was commonly defined by a fixed family income standard. In 1965 Molly Orshansky proposed a poverty measure based on current family income but with poverty lines that varied by family size, age composition, and farm/nonfarm status. While wealth was not explicitly included in the Orshansky measure, thresholds were set lower for both farm families and elderly households partly because of the greater frequency of home ownership (thus greater home equity wealth and associated housing services) for these groups than the general population.[2]

Later in the 1960s B. A. Weisbrod and W. L. Hansen explicitly accounted for wealth in measuring poverty (Weisbrod and Hansen 1968). They measured a family's economic position by current income plus the annual annuity value of net worth, a measure which we refer to as the WH measure. Based on 1962 data and using a fixed $3,000 poverty line for both current family income and WH, Weisbrod and Hansen found both a lower incidence of poverty and a younger age distribution of poverty households under the WH measure than under the simple income measure. J. Habib, M. Kohn, and R. Lerman applied the Weisbrod-Hansen technique by examining the distributions of income, wealth, and the combined WH measure in estimating poverty status in Israel over the 1963-1964 period (Habib, Kohn, and Lerman 1977). Adopting poverty lines that were 40 percent of the median for each measure of resources, they found that the composition of poverty by age, period of immigration, and country of origin was significantly different when measured by WH rather than by income alone. They also estimated the degree of overlap between measures, isolating groups counted as poor by more than one measure.

The research presented in this chapter applies the Weisbrod-Hansen methodology to estimate the size and demographic composition of poverty in rural and urban areas. In addition to its locational focus, this effort differs from prior studies of wealth and poverty status in several respects.

First, estimates of income-based and WH-based poverty were based on more recent data, the 1983 SCF. Second, poverty thresholds were adjusted for family size and composition, in contrast to the single poverty income limit used in the original Weisbrod-Hansen study. Third, we extended analysis of the composition of rural and urban poverty by the income and WH measures to numerous demographic characteristics; Weisbrod and Hansen limited their attention to the age dimension. We estimate both the total and independent effects of all demographic variables using crosstabulations and regression analysis. Finally, as in the Habib et al. study, we examine those considered poor by both measures, but again extend this analysis to several demographic characteristics of interest.

## DATA AND METHODOLOGY

The 1983 SCF contains detailed information on the balance sheets of 4,103 households nationwide. We removed a supplemental sample of 438 high-income households (unlikely to be helpful in analyzing poverty and low-income households)[3] and 156 households containing unrelated individuals (because of data limitations),[4] leaving us with a sample of 3,509 families. Properly weighted, this sample is designed to represent all families in the coterminous United States except persons housed on military installations or in institutional quarters. A locational code indicated residence in central cities, suburban areas (metropolitan areas outside central cities), areas adjacent to suburbs (outside suburban boundaries but within fifty miles of the central business district of a central city), and rural areas. The rural population, all persons living more than fifty miles from a central city and not in a suburb, was 14.5 percent of the weighted sample. With information from the SCF on income and wealth, assets and debts, location, and a wide range of other demographic characteristics of surveyed households, we determined poverty status by both the traditional income measure and our version of the WH income/wealth measure.

Poverty status under the conventional income definition is determined by 1982 family income and composition.[5] We use INC to refer to the income level and resulting poverty designation used for this conventional measure. A family was in or out of poverty under the INC measure according to whether its current income fell below, or above, the appropriate census poverty threshold.[6]

To determine a family's poverty status under the Weisbrod-Hansen income/wealth definition, we defined its WH value as the sum that could be spent annually so that all its wealth is consumed in its lifetime:

$$WH = Y + NW*A,$$

where Y is income net of the yield from net worth, NW is net worth, and A is the annuity value of one dollar of net worth. This net income measure Y differs from the income measure used to determine income-based poverty status in that Y excludes all returns on wealth holding. In addition to deducting capital gains, Y excludes income from individual retirement accounts (IRA) or Keogh accounts, dividends, interest, and rental income.[7] These are reflected in the annuity value of net worth and would otherwise be counted twice in the measure of WH. Net worth is gross assets of the household (including value of businesses owned and net present value of pensions) minus total household debts (including real estate and consumer debt).[8] The annuity value of net worth (A) depends on life expectancy of the family head and/or spouse. It is calculated on the assumption that net wealth becomes zero upon the death of both husband and wife, and that a family headed by a surviving spouse consumes at a rate of two-thirds of the original family unit.[9]

Poverty thresholds used with the new WH measure were adjusted upward from INC levels to reflect the change from an implicit to an explicit consideration of net worth.[10] We calibrated WH thresholds to replicate the poverty count of 34.5 million persons based on official 1983 poverty income thresholds, adjusted so that their relative levels are unchanged.[11] While the overall size and rate of WH poverty is the same as for INC poverty using this method, the composition of this poverty population may be quite different.

What effects do we expect that adding wealth to the poverty measure would have on the location of poverty and on the composition of rural and urban poverty? The expected net effect on rural/urban location is unclear because, as previously noted, rural areas have lower median wealth than do urban areas but a higher proportion of owners, older households, farmers, and self-employed individuals. When urban is split into large (metropolitan area over 2 million people) and small central cities, suburbs of large and small central cities, and areas adjacent to suburbs, differences in tenure among these categories are expected to result in differences in poverty status under the alternative measures. Central cities generally have a higher proportion of renters than less densely populated suburbs and adjacent areas, so that including wealth in the poverty measure may increase poverty rates in central cities and decrease them in suburban and outlying areas. However, the likely impact of wealth other than housing equity on WH poverty was harder to anticipate since the locational distribution of non-housing wealth is not well understood.

Age was expected to have a marked effect on the composition of both rural and urban poverty under the alternative measures. Since older persons tend to hold more wealth (much of it in the form of home equity) and have shorter life expectancies (increasing the annuity value of any given amount of wealth), we expected the WH measure to define a younger poverty population than did the income measure. This would be consistent with the findings of the Weisbrod-Hansen and Habib et al. studies. Also, lower poverty rates were expected from owners (compared to renters) and farmers (compared to other occupations) under the WH measure, since these groups tend to have more wealth. Recipients of public assistance tend to lack assets and generally must have limited assets to qualify for benefits. Thus they were expected to have a higher poverty rate under the WH measure. One might also expect families headed by females, nonwhites, and the unemployed to have lower than average net worth and thus be more often in poverty under the WH measure.

For most other demographic characteristics, the expected impact of a wealth-adjusted poverty measure was more difficult to postulate. Further, the total or uncontrolled effects on poverty status, for families with these characteristics, are often related to differences in age or tenure but with potentially offsetting influences. For example, married families with both spouses present or with two or more children are more likely to own their home than are other households, but they may also have accumulated more debts. Those in poor health may be those who are less capable of working, which may result in drawing down their wealth, but may more likely be older persons, who tend to have relatively high net wealth. The less educated may have fewer educational debts but may have found it more difficult to accumulate assets because of relatively low wages. Whether the population in WH-based poverty will be significantly different from that in INC poverty for each of these subgroups is unclear a priori for both rural and urban areas. Finally, we had no specific expectations of how these factors would tend to be associated with the level in poverty by both measures (to be referred to as those in "hard-core" poverty).

## FINDINGS

Nationally, 34.5 million persons (15.6 percent of the population) were in poverty in 1982 by the conventional income measure (Table 1.1). Of these, 87 percent, or 30 million persons, were the hard-core poor, also classified in poverty by the WH measure. While the total in WH poverty was equal to the INC poverty total (by our method of defining WH), 13 percent (4.5 million persons) of those in INC poverty were not in poverty by the WH measure.[12] In this section we examine to what extent the differences in the two poverty populations are systematically related to locational or demographic differences.

In analyzing poverty by location, we find large variation in poverty rates and some differences between those considered poor under the alternative poverty measures. As shown in Figure 1.1 and in Table 1.2, by either measure poverty was much higher in rural areas (21.1 percent poverty rate) than in the United States as a whole (15.6 percent) or in all urban areas (14.7 percent).[13] However, including wealth in the poverty definition did not change rural or urban poverty rates in net terms. This might seem surprising since a shift from INC to WH measurement would have the largest impact in rural areas, with mean WH 41 percent above mean INC (Table 1.3). But

**Table 1.1**
**Distribution of Poverty and Nonpoverty Groups under Alternative**
**Poverty Measures**

|                  |        | WH measure | | |
|------------------|--------|------------|-----------|-----------|
|                  |        | Not in poverty | In poverty | Totals |
| INC measure      | Not in poverty | 181.8 (82.4) | 4.4 (2.0) | 186.2 (84.4) |
|                  | In poverty | 4.5 (2.1) | 30.0 (13.6) | 34.5 (15.6) |
|                  | Totals | 186.3 (84.4) | 34.4 (15.6) | 220.7 (100.0) |

Source: Tabulations from 1983 Survey of Consumer
  Finances
Top numbers are in millions of persons; bottom
  numbers in parentheses are percent of total US
  population.

in rural areas this greater wealth seemed to be less frequently held by those in poverty by INC. It was suggested earlier that the older age distribution and lower median wealth in rural areas may have offsetting impacts on WH poverty rates. In fact, the various offsetting factors exactly canceled each other, leaving INC and WH poverty rates identical. In nonfarm rural America, however, poverty by the WH measure was slightly higher than by the conventional measure (Figure 1.2, Table 1.4).

Our breakdown of locations in urban America (where by our definition 85.5 percent of the population lives) into five categories reveals that rural poverty rates were above those of some urban areas and below those of others. Large cities experienced both the most and least severe poverty in their centers and suburbs respectively. The WH poverty measure showed even larger economic differences between city centers and suburbs than did the conventional INC measure (Figure 1.1, Table 1.2). By INC, these large central cities had poverty rates 4.4 times those of the suburbs; by WH, central city poverty was over 6 times the suburban level.

By both measures, the second and third highest poverty rates were in rural areas (21 percent INC and WH) and central cities of under 2 million population (18 percent INC and WH). While including wealth did not change the poverty rates for these areas, the poverty rate in suburbs of small central cities grew from 13 percent to 14 percent after accounting for

**Figure 1.1**
**Location: Income and Weisbrod-Hansen Poverty Measures**

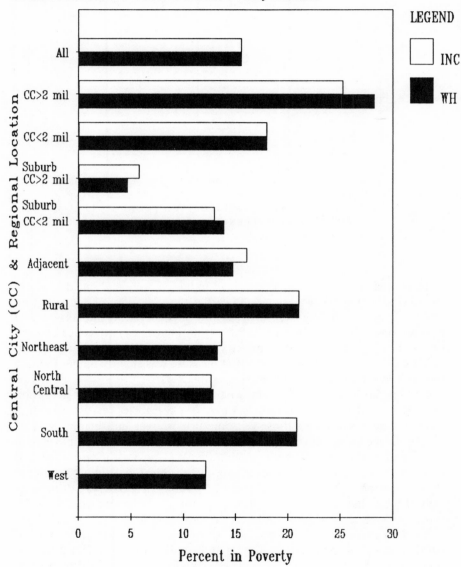

**Table 1.2**
**Poverty Rates by Location under INC and WH Measures**

| Location | Income-based (INC) poverty | WH-based poverty | Ratio of WH to INC poverty | Ratio of INC hardcore to INC poverty |
|---|---|---|---|---|
| | Percent | Percent | Ratio | Ratio |
| U.S. TOTAL | 15.6 | 15.6 | 1.00 | 0.87 |
| RURAL/URBAN STATUS | | | | |
| Rural | 21.1 | 21.1 | 1.00 | 0.86 |
| Urban | 14.7 | 14.7 | 1.00 | 0.87 |
| CENTRAL CITY (CC) LOCATIONAL STATUS | | | | |
| CC > 2 million | 25.3 | 28.3 | 1.12 | 0.95 |
| CC < 2 million | 18.0 | 18.0 | 1.00 | 0.92 |
| Suburb of CC > 2 million | 5.8 | 4.7 | 0.81 | 0.75 |
| Suburb of CC < 2 million | 13.0 | 13.9 | 1.07 | 0.86 |
| Adjacent | 16.1 | 14.8 | 0.92 | 0.81 |
| Rural | 21.1 | 21.1 | 1.00 | 0.86 |
| REGION | | | | |
| Northeast | 13.7 | 13.3 | 0.97 | 0.88 |
| North Central | 12.7 | 12.9 | 1.02 | 0.87 |
| South | 20.9 | 20.9 | 1.00 | 0.88 |
| West | 12.2 | 12.2 | 1.00 | 0.84 |

Source: Tabulations from 1983 Survey of Consumer Finances
The "hardcore" poor are those in poverty by both INC and WH measures.

**Table 1.3**
**Mean INC and WH by Location**

------------------------------------------------------------

| Location | Mean INC | Mean WH | Ratio of Mean WH to INC |
|---|---|---|---|
| | Dollars | | Ratio |
| | ------- | | ----- |
| U.S. TOTAL | 26,101 | 33,687 | 1.29 |
| RURAL/URBAN STATUS | | | |
| Rural | 20,737 | 29,342 | 1.41 |
| Urban | 27,041 | 34,449 | 1.27 |
| CENTRAL CITY (CC) | | | |
| LOCATIONAL STATUS | | | |
| CC > 2 million | 23,743 | 27,078 | 1.14 |
| CC < 2 million | 23,251 | 29,127 | 1.25 |
| Suburb of CC>2 million | 38,726 | 48,240 | 1.25 |
| Suburb of CC<2 million | 27,113 | 36,525 | 1.35 |
| Adjacent | 22,561 | 29,864 | 1.32 |
| Rural | 20,737 | 29,342 | 1.41 |
| REGION | | | |
| Northeast | 29,430 | 36,485 | 1.24 |
| North Central | 26,095 | 34,334 | 1.32 |
| South | 22,543 | 28,003 | 1.24 |
| West | 28,605 | 39,637 | 1.39 |

------------------------------------------------------------

Source: Tabulations from 1983 Survey of Consumer Finances

wealth. Unlike the situation for large cities, this narrowed the difference between central city and suburban poverty rates.

At nearly 21 percent by both measures, the South had the highest rate of poverty of all regions (Figure 1.1 and Table 1.2). Following, in order but with very similar poverty rates, were the Northeast, the North Central, and the West. The South also had the lowest family mean value of INC and WH of all regions (Table 1.3). Accounting for wealth in the poverty measure made little difference in the regional distribution of poverty.

Our analysis of rural and urban poverty by demographic characteristics begins with age, a variable having a widely acknowledged associaton with the distribution of wealth. Poverty rates are lowest in the middle (35-64) age categories and highest in the youngest and oldest categories by both measures and in both rural and urban areas (Figure 1.3 and Table 1.4). However, poverty under the WH measure has a younger age distribution than under INC, as expected. Beyond the age of forty-five, the poverty rates

**Figure 1.2**
**Selected Family Head Characteristics: Income and Weisbrod-Hansen**
**Poverty Measures**

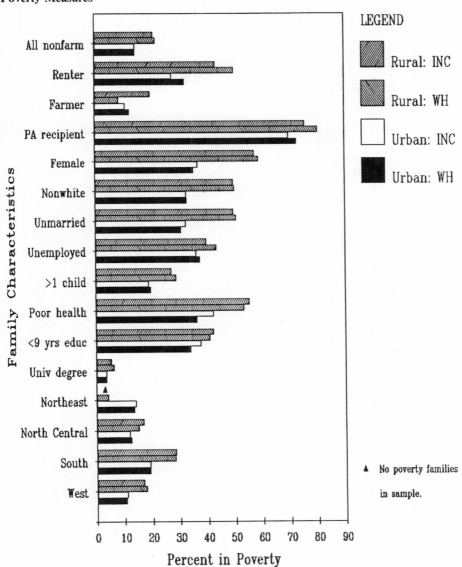

Table 1.4

Rural and Urban Poverty Rates under INC and WH Measures for Various
Demographic Characteristics of Family Head

| Characteristic | Rural | | | | Urban | | | |
|---|---|---|---|---|---|---|---|---|
| | Income-based (INC) poverty | WH-based poverty | Ratio of WH to INC poverty | Ratio of hardcore to INC poverty | Income-based (INC) poverty | WH-based poverty | Ratio of WH to INC poverty | Ratio of hardcore to INC poverty |
| | Percent | | | Ratio | Percent | | | Ratio |
| U.S. TOTAL | 21.1 | 21.1 | 1.00 | 0.86 | 14.7 | 14.7 | 1.00 | 0.87 |
| U.S. NONFARM TOTAL | 21.2 | 22.0 | 1.04 | 0.89 | 14.7 | 14.6 | 1.00 | 0.87 |
| AGE | | | | | | | | |
| <25 | 31.8 | 36.3 | 1.14 | 1.00 | 23.6 | 30.8 | 1.30 | 0.98 |
| 25-34 | 25.1 | 29.9 | 1.19 | 0.95 | 16.3 | 18.0 | 1.11 | 0.99 |
| 35-44 | 14.1 | 15.0 | 1.06 | 0.95 | 11.5 | 11.6 | 1.01 | 0.89 |
| 45-54 | 21.9 | 20.4 | 0.94 | 0.83 | 13.2 | 11.8 | 0.89 | 0.84 |
| 55-64 | 11.5 | 8.8 | 0.76 | 0.63 | 13.3 | 11.8 | 0.89 | 0.80 |
| 65-74 | 21.8 | 16.2 | 0.74 | 0.71 | 14.2 | 11.0 | 0.78 | 0.65 |
| >=75 | 37.3 | 30.2 | 0.81 | 0.73 | 27.9 | 22.1 | 0.79 | 0.68 |
| TENURE | | | | | | | | |
| Owner | 11.9 | 8.6 | 0.73 | 0.64 | 8.6 | 6.5 | 0.76 | 0.71 |
| Renter | 43.5 | 50.1 | 1.15 | 0.99 | 27.8 | 32.5 | 1.17 | 0.99 |
| OCCUPATION, FULL TIME WORKERS | | | | | | | | |
| All full time workers | 10.7 | 11.2 | 1.04 | 0.79 | 6.8 | 7.4 | 1.08 | 0.87 |
| Professional,technical | 4.1 | 4.1 | 1.00 | 1.00 | 2.4 | 2.7 | 1.14 | 0.90 |
| Manager,administrative | 0.0 | 0.0 | - | | 2.2 | 1.3 | 0.59 | 0.59 |
| Self-employed manager | 9.1 | 6.5 | 0.71 | 0.71 | 6.3 | 3.7 | 0.58 | 0.58 |
| Sales,clerical | 4.9 | 6.0 | 1.22 | 1.00 | 6.1 | 7.0 | 1.15 | 0.85 |
| Crafts,protective service | 12.8 | 9.4 | 0.73 | 0.73 | 6.0 | 6.7 | 1.12 | 0.92 |
| Labor,service | 16.3 | 23.3 | 1.43 | 0.92 | 13.0 | 14.6 | 1.13 | 0.91 |
| Farmer | 20.0 | 8.7 | 0.43 | 0.43 | 11.0 | 12.5 | 1.13 | 0.79 |

| | | | | | | | | |
|---|---|---|---|---|---|---|---|---|
| PUBLIC ASSISTANCE RECIPIENTS | | | | | | | | |
| Recipients | 75.8 | 80.3 | 1.06 | 1.00 | 69.8 | 72.8 | 1.04 | 0.97 |
| Nonrecipients | 10.8 | 9.9 | 0.92 | 0.68 | 7.9 | 7.6 | 0.95 | 0.77 |
| SEX | | | | | | | | |
| Male | 14.0 | 13.7 | 0.98 | 0.78 | 9.7 | 10.0 | 1.03 | 0.86 |
| Female | 57.4 | 58.9 | 1.03 | 0.96 | 37.0 | 35.4 | 0.96 | 0.89 |
| RACE | | | | | | | | |
| White | 14.3 | 14.3 | 1.00 | 0.78 | 9.5 | 9.4 | 0.99 | 0.83 |
| Nonwhite | 49.9 | 50.1 | 1.00 | 0.96 | 32.8 | 33.0 | 1.01 | 0.91 |
| MARITAL STATUS | | | | | | | | |
| Married | 13.5 | 13.3 | 0.98 | 0.79 | 8.8 | 9.3 | 1.06 | 0.86 |
| Unmarried | 49.9 | 50.7 | 1.02 | 0.94 | 32.6 | 30.9 | 0.95 | 0.88 |
| NUMBER OF CHILDREN | | | | | | | | |
| 0 | 18.8 | 16.8 | 0.89 | 0.80 | 10.7 | 9.2 | 0.86 | 0.73 |
| 1 | 13.1 | 13.6 | 1.04 | 0.86 | 13.3 | 14.0 | 1.05 | 0.88 |
| 2 or more | 27.3 | 29.0 | 1.06 | 0.90 | 19.0 | 19.9 | 1.05 | 0.94 |
| HEALTH | | | | | | | | |
| Excellent | 13.6 | 14.7 | 1.08 | 0.89 | 7.9 | 8.5 | 1.08 | 0.89 |
| Good | 14.7 | 15.1 | 1.03 | 0.86 | 13.7 | 14.3 | 1.05 | 0.89 |
| Fair | 34.4 | 32.4 | 0.94 | 0.82 | 26.2 | 24.9 | 0.95 | 0.88 |
| Poor | 55.3 | 53.4 | 0.97 | 0.88 | 42.3 | 36.4 | 0.86 | 0.77 |
| EMPLOYMENT STATUS | | | | | | | | |
| Working (full or part time) | 13.6 | 14.4 | 1.05 | 0.84 | 7.9 | 8.3 | 1.05 | 0.88 |
| Unemployed | 39.9 | 43.6 | 1.09 | 1.00 | 36.2 | 37.6 | 1.04 | 0.90 |
| Retired,student,housewife | 38.9 | 35.6 | 0.92 | 0.85 | 33.2 | 30.9 | 0.93 | 0.85 |
| EDUCATION | | | | | | | | |
| 0-8 yrs | 42.3 | 41.1 | 0.97 | 0.86 | 37.8 | 34.1 | 0.90 | 0.83 |
| 9-12 yrs | 36.0 | 37.9 | 1.05 | 0.97 | 28.1 | 29.0 | 1.03 | 0.92 |
| HS diploma | 12.7 | 12.7 | 1.00 | 0.78 | 12.8 | 13.6 | 1.06 | 0.88 |
| Some college | 9.1 | 7.8 | 0.86 | 0.71 | 7.3 | 7.4 | 1.01 | 0.86 |
| College degree | 5.6 | 6.5 | 1.16 | 0.75 | 3.7 | 3.7 | 1.02 | 0.82 |
| REGION | | | | | | | | |
| Northeast | 0.0 | 4.3 | - | | 14.2 | 13.7 | 0.96 | 0.88 |
| North Central | 16.9 | 15.2 | 0.90 | 0.66 | 12.0 | 12.5 | 1.04 | 0.91 |
| South | 28.7 | 28.4 | 0.99 | 0.88 | 19.2 | 19.2 | 1.00 | 0.87 |
| West | 16.9 | 18.0 | 1.06 | 0.99 | 11.0 | 10.7 | 0.97 | 0.78 |

13

are lower by the WH than the INC measure, as shown by the ratio of WH to INC of below one (Table 1.4, columns 3 and 7). Also, the share of hard-core poor in the INC poverty population generally falls with age (Table 1.4, columns 4 and 8). As discussed earlier, a younger age distribution in poverty under the WH measure is expected since older households have typically accumulated more assets than have younger households, and current income tends to fall with age in the upper age categories (Lerman and Lerman 1986). In addition, older households in INC-based poverty tend to have incomes closer to the poverty line than most other poor households (Weicher 1987). From this, one might conclude that the conventional INC definition overstates the economic problems of older groups and under-states those of younger groups. However, even by the WH measure, poverty rates are high for older persons. In both rural and urban areas, the oldest age group (over 74) has a WH poverty rate second only to that of the youngest group (under 25). In rural areas, poverty rates begin rising with increasing age at a younger threshold. They are significantly higher for persons over sixty-five than for the next younger age group, but substan-tially the same in urban areas. Additionally, the ratio of hard-core poor to those in INC poverty rises with age in the oldest two age groups in rural areas and in the oldest group in urban areas.

Renters had far higher poverty rates than did home owners by both measures in both rural and urban areas. As expected, taking account of wealth caused poverty to appear even more severe among renters and less severe among owners. While the INC poverty rate of urban renters was 3.2 times that of home owners (3.7 times in rural areas), it was 5 times as high (5.8 times in rural areas) under WH.

Among rural families with the head and/or the spouse working full time (69 percent of the rural sample), two occupational groups with higher than average INC poverty had below average WH poverty: crafts and protective service workers and farmers and farm managers (Table 1.4). The decline in measured poverty among rural farmers, which probably occurred because many farmers held relatively more property assets, was over 50 percent.[14] Poverty among laborers and service employees in rural areas, however, was much higher by the WH measure. In urban areas, except for two managerial categories, WH-based poverty was over 10 percent higher than conventional levels for all occupational groups, which may reflect a younger full-time working population in urban areas.

Public assistance recipients and unemployed workers, who probably had few assets, showed increases in poverty under WH in both rural and urban areas (Table 1.4 and Figure 1.2). Results were mixed for females and non-whites, the two other groups hypothesized in the discussion of data and methodology to sustain poverty increases under the WH measure because of relatively low wealth. The poverty rate of female-headed households did increase in rural areas but decreased in urban areas. No change was found

**Figure 1.3**
**Age of Family Head: Income and Weisbrod-Hansen Poverty Measures**

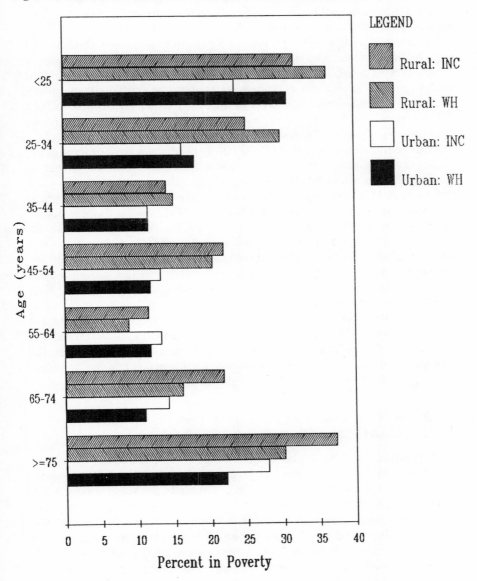

in measured poverty for nonwhite households in either rural or urban areas. Both of these groups had substantially higher poverty than the national average by either measure.

Poverty by both measures was much more frequent among unmarried than married households. While this difference narrowed under the WH measure in urban areas, in rural areas it widened slightly.

Poverty was particularly high for families with two or more children and grew higher after accounting for wealth in both rural and urban areas. A closely related result is that in both rural and urban areas more children were in poverty under the WH measure (Table 1.5). Although the urban percentage of children in poverty was higher by either measure, a shift to WH increased children in poverty more in rural areas (6.4 percent increase) than in urban areas (5.5 percent increase).

Health condition as reported by the family head was a major factor in the incidence of poverty. By either measure, poverty increased as health deteriorated, no doubt partly because poor health means inability to work and to earn. However, the difference in poverty rates between healthy and unhealthy households was less under WH, probably because those in poorer health are also often older households, who tend to have higher net worth.

Poverty declined significantly as educational level rose. Although poverty was highest among those with less than nine years of education, accounting for wealth produced a decline in measured poverty in this group in both rural and urban areas. A possible explanation is again age-related: the least educated are often older.

Poverty rates were higher in the rural areas of all regions (except the Northeast, which lacked observations). Rural poverty in the West and North Central regions were equal by the INC measure. However, by the WH measure, the poverty population increased 6 percent in the West but fell 10 percent in the North Central region.

## COMPARING POVERTY MEASURES USING MULTIVARIATE ANALYSIS

The findings presented above were based on crosstabulations, which provide the total or uncontrolled effect of each locational and demographic variable in rural and urban poverty status. However, for some applications, we may be interested in how each variable independently affects poverty status. For example, part of the wide difference in poverty rates between those in excellent health and those in poor health may be attributed to age; that is, those in poor health are more often elderly, and elderly households have higher than average poverty rates. A multivariate regression analysis was thus performed to estimate the independent or controlled effects of numerous variables. It also determined whether such effects were statistically

**Table 1.5**
**Children in Poverty**

| Poverty measure | Rural | | | | Urban | | | |
|---|---|---|---|---|---|---|---|---|
| | Children in poverty | Total persons in poverty | Ratio of children to total | | Children in poverty | Total persons in poverty | Ratio of children to total | |
| | Thousands | | Percent | | Thousands | | Percent | |
| INC | 2,414 | 6,736 | 35.8 | | 10,848 | 27,777 | 39.1 | |
| WH | 2,570 | 6,733 | 38.2 | | 11,420 | 27,679 | 41.3 | |

Source: Tabulations from 1983 Survey of Consumer Finances

significant, and where appropriate, whether the effect in rural areas differed significantly from that in urban areas.

Locational and demographic variables (recoded as zero-one dummy variables) plus rural/urban interaction terms were regressed on the difference between the WH measure and INC. This yielded the average dollar and percent margin of WH over INC attributable to each variable. Positive (negative) coefficients indicate that the incidence of poverty is probably lowered (raised) under the WH measure. Coefficients for farmer, locational categories, and regions represent increments to the overall (WH – INC) difference. Coefficients for each of the remaining variables other than the rural interaction terms (labeled "rural and" in Table 1.6) represent the urban increments to the national (WH – INC) difference, while "rural and" coefficients must be added to the respective urban increment to yield the variable's rural increment. The separate rural effect (– $266) must also be added when comparing an item's rural effect to the national level, but not when comparing its effect to the overall rural level. Since our interest was focused on the poor and near poor, only families below either median WH or median INC were used in the regressions. This narrowed the income range analyzed to one that is more likely to be linear and thus appropriately treated with this linear technique.

Illustrating a result from Table 1.6, we found that the urban elderly, compared to all nonelderly households, had an additional margin of WH over INC of $1,811. This margin was 53 percent of the mean differential of $3,413 for the entire regression sample and was significantly different from zero. In rural areas, the elderly effect was much larger and significantly different from the urban effect. Being rural and elderly added an average $6,576 to the national (WH – INC) difference ($1,811 plus the interaction effect of $5,031 plus the overall rural effect of – $266). These positive elderly effects are consistent with earlier crosstabulation findings that the elderly have lower poverty under the WH measure. The regression results show that this conclusion continues to hold even after controlling for other factors.

In addition to the elderly, home owners, farmers, high school graduates, retirees, those not receiving public assistance, and residents of Western states also appeared less likely to be considered poor (i.e., had a significantly larger excess of WH over INC than those in the opposite grouping). All other factors equal (including age), urban retirees overall fared better by the WH measure, but rural retirees did not. However, most retirees are elderly, and for this age group the (WH – INC) increment of rural retirees was high as was the situation for all rural elderly. Significant at the 0.15 level was the negative impact on WH of poor health in rural areas. Being in poor health in rural areas lowered the excess of WH over INC by $2,674 (– $2,490 plus – $184) compared to rural persons not in poor health.

Of course, the uncontrolled effects of variables in crosstabulations may

**Table 1.6**
**Regression Results: Effects of Demographic Variables on Differences between Poverty Measures**

| Variable | Effect on Excess of WH Measure Over INC | | Significance |
|---|---|---|---|
| | Dollar Effect | Effect as Ratio to Mean Difference | |
| Single | -574 | -0.17 | |
| Elderly (65+) | 1811 | 0.53 | *** |
| Male | 505 | 0.15 | |
| Married | -375 | -0.11 | |
| Owner | 4422 | 1.30 | *** |
| Farmer | 19880 | 5.82 | *** |
| White | 389 | 0.11 | |
| HS grad | 2036 | 0.60 | *** |
| Poor health | -184 | -0.05 | |
| Unemployed | 95 | 0.03 | |
| Retired | 1993 | 0.58 | *** |
| Pub assist recip | -1332 | -0.39 | ** |
| 2+ children | -689 | -0.20 | |
| Large cent city | -43 | -0.01 | |
| Small cent city | -10 | -0.00 | |
| Suburb large city | 467 | 0.14 | |
| Suburb small city | -278 | -0.08 | |
| Rural | -266 | -0.08 | |
| North Central | 565 | 0.17 | |
| West | 1279 | 0.37 | ** |
| South | -106 | -0.03 | |
| Rural and: | | | |
| Single | -416 | -0.12 | |
| Elderly | 5032 | 1.47 | ** |
| Male | 1462 | 0.43 | |
| Married | -1242 | -0.36 | |
| Owner | 1151 | 0.34 | |
| White | 624 | 0.18 | |
| HS grad | -1059 | -0.31 | |
| Poor health | -2490 | -0.73 | + |
| Unemployed | 46 | 0.01 | |
| Retired | -2657 | -0.78 | * |
| Pub assist recip | 644 | 0.19 | |
| 2+ children | 247 | 0.07 | |
| Intercept term | -1906 | -0.56 | *** |

OLS regression run on all families below median WH or INC
   (mean excess of WH over INC for this group = $3,413)
Dependent variable = WH measure minus income
R squared = .23
n = 1897
Significance at .01 level = ***      at .10 level = *
              at .05 level = **      at .15 level = +

well be quite different from estimates of their controlled effects based on regression results. For example, several characteristics found in the crosstabulations to have very different poverty rates under the two measures show insignificant differences between WH and INC in the regression findings. For example, residents of large central cities had higher poverty rates by WH than by INC, but they did not have a significantly lower (WH – INC) differential than all other households, ceteris paribus. One explanation is that large central cities may have relatively high proportions of renters, workers, nonelderly persons, or those receiving public assistance (i.e., groups that have higher poverty under the WH measure), whereas the regression results control for these effects. Another explanation is that the crosstabulation and regression approaches do not necessarily correspond to one another. That is, there may be many families in large central cities whose poverty status is different under the two measures but whose absolute (WH – INC) differential is small.

## CONCLUSIONS

Poverty rates and composition of the poverty population vary substantially by rural/urban and regional location. Yet the omission of wealth from the current income-based INC poverty measure can bias rural/urban comparisons. In this chapter, we examined the effects on the distribution of poverty that result from modifying the INC poverty measure to include the annuity value of household net worth.

Both rural and urban poverty populations are changed somewhat by the new WH income/wealth measure. About one-seventh of INC poor (14 percent in rural and 13 percent in urban areas) were not in WH poverty; a like number of nonpoor were redefined as poor by the WH measure.

With reference to all U.S. families for locational factors and to all rural families for other characteristics, the following differences between poverty measures of greater than 5 percent were found.[15] Compared to the INC poor, those in poverty by the WH measure are more often residents of the West or large central cities or suburbs of small central cities, families with two or more children, and families headed by a person who is younger (under 45); a renter; a full-time service, sales, or clerical employee; a public assistance recipient; in excellent health; unemployed; or a college graduate. Those in poverty by the INC measure, as compared to the WH poor, were more often residents of the North Central region or suburbs of large central cities or areas adjacent to suburbs; families with no children; and families headed by a retiree, student, home owner, farmer, full-time craft or protective service employee, housewife, or a person with some college or with less than nine years of education.

Multivariate analysis suggested that age, home ownership, farm employment, education, retirement status, public assistance participation, and residence in the West were independently significant factors in explaining divergence of the two poverty measures. Age, retirement status, and perhaps poor health also had significantly different influences in rural than in urban areas, although rural residence itself was not an important factor in explaining WH and INC differences.

This research provides only partial explanations of what lies behind the current locational distribution of poverty. Large differences in the size and makeup of poverty by region and rural/urban location remain unexplained. While providing a current cash value, which considers the value of assets, the WH measure falls short of fully accounting for a person's financial well-being (Lerman and Mikesell 1988). Also, the SCF's sample size limits possible analysis of smaller subgroups. However, this research does provide some valuable insights on how an alternative poverty measure can change our view of who is poor in rural and urban America. The tabulation of poverty by various locational and demographic characteristics also uncovered some interesting, and sometimes unexpected, details about the poor.

## NOTES

The authors wish to thank Dan Milkove, Pat Sullivan, Ellen Burkhart, and Steven Pressman for their helpful comments on an earlier version of this paper.

1. For example, in 1983 the correlation coefficient between income and wealth for all U.S. households was 0.49 and slightly higher in rural areas (0.61). If income is measured net of the yield from net worth (i.e., if capital gains, IRA income, dividends, interest, and rent are removed from total income), the income-wealth correlation between income and wealth of all families falls to 0.26 (all estimates based on 1983 Survey of Consumer Finances data).

2. For farmers, lower thresholds also accounted for the value of food produced and consumed on the typical farm.

3. Information on location was not available for those in the high-income sample. Some of our empirical work was run for the entire U.S. sample including the high-income sample, and results were unchanged.

4. While the poverty status of a person living with his or her family is determined by family income, for an unrelated individual, poverty status is determined by his or her own income, according to census procedure. However, data were not available on family income for households containing unrelated individuals since income in the SCF was given for the entire household and not supplied for individual household members. Thus we removed households containing unrelated individuals (this group comprised less than 5 percent of the sample).

5. The official census income measure used in measuring poverty status is money income received in the previous calendar year by family members of the household from each of the following sources: wages and salaries, net self-employment income, dividends, interest income, rental income, alimony or child support payments received, retirement income, and public assistance benefits in money form. Capital gains and all in-kind income (e.g., food stamps) are not included. To arrive at this income measure using SCF data, we included income from all sources and deducted

capital gains and food stamp income. Food stamp income was estimated as 27 percent of total public assistance income (based on Bureau of Economic Analysis data on the proportion of total welfare income represented by food stamps).

6. Separate official census poverty thresholds were also defined for one- and two-person households with an elderly head. Because the elderly and nonelderly thresholds were nearly identical, we chose not to make this adjustment and averaged them into single thresholds for these household sizes.

7. In the SCF, some income reported as self-employment income may actually reflect returns to owned business assets, raising the potential for double counting with the WH measure. In compensation, for families reporting both self-employment income greater than $30,000 (the 75th percentile of self-employment earners) and also owning a business worth over $134,644 (the 75th percentile of present values of all family-owned businesses), self-employment income was reduced to half its reported value.

8. Because of the bankruptcy option, we reset all negative net worth values to zero. However, of the 2.0 percent of total cases in which a family not in income-based poverty fell into poverty under WH, none had negative net worth. Thus this adjustment had no impact on our findings.

9. Hence for a single individual,

$$A = \frac{r}{1 - (1+r)^{-n}}$$

where r is the rate of interest and n is the life expectancy of the individual or of both spouses if they have equal life expectancy. Estimates of life expectancy were based upon U.S. Department of Health and Social Services estimates by age (from sixteen to ninety-six years old) and sex. If one spouse has greater life expectancy $(m > n)$ than the other, A is given by

$$A = \frac{r}{1 - (1/3)(1+r)^{-n} - (2/3)(1+r)^{-m}}$$

An interest rate of 8 percent was used to annuitize net worth for the WH measures presented in this report. That selection represents a nominal rate of return that could be expected on an annuity. We investigated the potential differences with 4- and 12-percent rates and concluded that the general findings were not affected. For instance, over 95 percent of the poverty population as defined using a 4-percent interest rate are the same persons defined as poor at 8 percent. The method of defining the WH poverty population ensures that their total number is not affected by the selected interest rate.

10. A common view is that current poverty income limits were originally set to allow for some "normal" or "typical" level of family assets (Weisbrod 1965). Under this interpretation, WH poverty thresholds should be higher than current income thresholds since WH includes family assets.

11. This poverty count of 34.5 million was calculated using our data base and 1983 official poverty thresholds, closely approximating the official 1983 poverty count of 34.4 million. The former "synthetic" figure was used rather than the official figure so that both income and WH poverty totals are based on the same data base (SCF).

In addition, smaller households would tend to cluster into the lower rankings of WH and larger households into the higher rankings. Since larger households need more resources to feed their members at subsistence levels, we weighted the WH by a factor equal to the reciprocal of its official poverty threshold, where these factors are normalized to sum to one over all households. That is, let $t_i$ represent the official (income-based) poverty threshold for a particular family based on its size and composition. Let $r_i = (1/t_i)$, and $\bar{r}$ = mean of the $r_i$ over all families. Then weight this family's WH by

$$s_i = (r_i/\bar{r})$$

As noted in Habib, Kohn, and Lerman (1977), it is appropriate to adjust poverty lines of the WH measure for family size and composition if savings serve primarily to redistribute consumption over time for the existing family unit and not primarily to provide children with an inheritance or to provide for new family members.

12. In our sample "each household" represented on average about 71,000 people, and thus discontinuous jumps occurred in the cumulative total number of households ranked from lowest to highest by the WH measure. Since such a jump occurred at the WH poverty threshold, the estimate of the number in WH poverty (34.4 million) was slightly less than the number (34.5 million) in poverty under the conventional measure.

13. This rural/urban difference in poverty appears greater than that reported by Bentley (1987), who found that poverty was 18.3 percent in nonmetropolitan areas and 13.8 percent in metropolitan areas in 1983. However, nonmetropolitan America (representing about one-quarter of the total population) is more inclusive than our rural definition (which includes 14.5 percent of the U.S. population). Income-based poverty for our rural and adjacent areas combined (comprising 37 percent of U.S. population) was 18 percent.

14. Farm findings should be interpreted with caution because farm income can vary greatly from year to year, and the value of many agriculture related assets has fallen dramatically since 1983 (Lerman 1988).

15. This information is based on whether the ratios of WH to INC from column 3 of Table 1.4 (and column 3 of Table 1.2 for central city locational categories) are either below 0.96 or above 1.04. A similar comparison for urban families can be made from column 7 of Table 1.4.

## REFERENCES

Avery, R. B., G. E. Elliehausen, and G. B. Canner. 1984. "Survey of Consumer Finances, 1983." *Federal Reserve Bulletin* 70: 679-92.

Bentley, S. 1987. "Income Transfers, Taxes, and the Poor." *Rural Development Perspectives* 3: 30-33.

Council of Economic Advisors. 1965. "Some Economic Tasks of the Great Society." In *The Economics of Poverty,* edited by B. A. Weisbrod. Englewood Cliffs, N.J.: Prentice-Hall.

Habib, J., M. Kohn, and R. Lerman. 1977. "The Effect on Poverty Status in Israel of Considering Wealth and Variability of Income." *Review of Income and Wealth* 23: 17-38.

Lerman, D. L. 1988. "Rural Portfolios" Economic Research Service, U.S. Department of Agriculture. Unpublished paper.

Lerman, D. L., and R. I. Lerman. 1986. "Income from Owner-Occupied Housing and Income Inequality." *Urban Studies* 23: 323-31.

Lerman, D. L., and J. J. Mikesell. 1988. "Impacts of Adding Net Worth to the Poverty Definition." *Eastern Economic Journal* 14: 357-70.

Orshansky, M. 1965. "Counting the Poor: Another Look at the Poverty Profile." *Social Security Bulletin* 28: 3-29.

Sawhill, I. V. 1988. "Poverty in the U.S.: Why Is It So Persistent?" *Journal of Economic Literature* 26: 1073-119.

U.S. Bureau of the Census. 1984. *Characteristics of the Population Below the Poverty Level: 1982.* Current Population Reports, Series P-60, no. 144. Washington, D.C.: U.S. Government Printing Office.

Weicher, J. C. 1987. "Mismeasuring Poverty and Progress." *Cato Journal* 6: 715-30.

Weisbrod, B. A. 1965. "The Economics of Poverty: An American Paradox." In *The Economics of Poverty,* edited by B. A. Weisbrod. Englewood Cliffs, N.J.: Prentice-Hall.

Weisbrod, B. A., and W. L. Hansen. 1968. "An Income-Net Worth Approach to Measuring Economic Welfare." *American Economic Review* 58: 1315-29.

## 2
## Rural-Urban Differences in the Utilization and Ameliorative Effects of Welfare Programs

### LEIF JENSEN

### INTRODUCTION

Welfare programs such as Aid to Families with Dependent Children (AFDC) and general assistance (GA) were designed primarily to provide income security and alleviate poverty (Levitan 1985). Over the past decade or so, there has been increasing concern that welfare fosters dependency and fails to promote self-sufficiency through gainful employment (Murray 1984). These concerns have given rise to welfare reform proposals that emphasize remedial education, skill training, and job placement, and they have sparked considerable interest and new research on welfare dependency (e.g., Hopkins 1987). To some extent, the recent furor has blurred the original intent of welfare—to ameliorate poverty.

It is well known that poverty rates have been perennially higher in rural than urban areas of the United States (Jensen 1987), and this continues to be true today (Rodgers and Weiher 1986).[1] Despite this, many Americans perceive that poverty is predominantly an urban problem, and some have suggested that government poverty programs contain an urban bias (Hoppe 1980; Institute for Research on Poverty 1980; Watkins and Watkins 1984).

A partial explanation for this is simply that, compared to urban areas, rural poverty is much more geographically dispersed, rendering it less conspicuous. While this dispersion has led to a popular neglect of rural poverty, on a more practical level it restricts access of the rural poor to social services more readily available to the urban poor (Deavers, Hoppe, and Ross 1986). Despite the differences between metro and nonmetro poverty, the rural poor must rely on the same "safety net" as the urban.

A key feature of this safety net is the set of government welfare programs. The term "welfare" has been used to refer to a variety of programs. In this chapter, welfare income is that which derives from AFDC and GA.[2] Given the higher incidence of poverty in nonmetro areas, the comparative effectiveness of welfare programs in nonmetro versus metro America is an important policy issue. There is evidence that the rural poor are less likely to avail themselves of income transfer programs (Carlson, Lassey, and Lassey 1981), and that the ameliorative effect of welfare is less in rural than urban areas (Jensen 1987).

Accordingly, at a time when appreciable policy concern rests with welfare dependency, I seek to refocus attention on the degree to which welfare alleviates poverty by highlighting and explaining rural-urban differences in this ameliorative effect. The unit of analysis is the family, defined here as two or more persons living together who are related by blood, marriage, or adoption. Basic descriptive statistical techniques and multivariate methods are used to analyze data from the March 1987 Current Population Survey. First, basic measures of economic well-being among families in nonmetro and metro areas are discussed, and data for families in central cities are provided. This is followed by an investigation of rural-urban differences in the ability of welfare to alleviate poverty. Several measures of this ameliorative effect are considered. Multivariate methods are then used, first to decompose rural-urban differences in the ameliorative effect of welfare, and then to explain metro-nonmetro differences in the propensity of families to receive welfare benefits.

## DATA ANALYSIS

### Baseline Data

Before examining metro-nonmetro differences in the ameliorative effects of welfare programs, fundamental measures of economic well-being are presented in Table 2.1. This establishes an aggregate picture of rural-urban differences in the need for income security programs.

By comparing the first two columns of Table 2.1, it becomes apparent that economic deprivation is more prevalent in nonmetro than metro areas. The percent of families with income below the poverty threshold[3] is 15.2 and 10.1 in nonmetro and metro America, respectively. This gap holds for more severe depths of poverty as well. Over 10 percent of nonmetro families have income amounts below 75 percent of their poverty cutoff. Less than 7 percent of metro families are so deprived. That one in ten rural families has

**Table 2.1**
**Poverty and Welfare Receipt among Nonmetro and Metro Families**

|  | Nonmetro | Metro | |
|---|---|---|---|
|  | Total | Total | Central City |
| Percent of families with income below poverty line | 15.2 | 10.1* | 15.4 |
| Percent of families with income below .75 of poverty line | 10.3 | 6.9* | 11.2 |
| Percent of families with income below .5 of poverty line | 6.1 | 4.0* | 6.6 |
| Mean Total Family Income (1986 dollars) | $26,626 | $36,580* | $32,017* |
| Mean Total Family Earnings (1986 dollars) | $20,651 | $30,267* | $25,905* |
| Percent of families that received welfare income | 5.9 | 5.8 | 10.3* |
| Percent of poor families that received welfare income | 30.2 | 41.8* | 49.9* |
| Mean welfare income among recipient families | $2,928 | $3,652* | $3,911* |
| Total N (weighted[1]) | 9,704 | 32,589 | 10,177 |

* T-test with respect to nonmetro areas significant at p < .01.

[1] CPS weight is divided by mean weight to yield total N approximately equal to CPS sample size.

Source: March 1987 Current Population Survey, U.S. Census Bureau

a total income below this level (75 percent of $11,203 leaves $8,402 for a family of four) is startling considering the truly meager life-style afforded by an income so low. Several observers have documented the near impossibility of making ends meet with a poverty-level income (Schiller 1980); 75 percent of this income can only entail much greater difficulty.

Considering a yet deeper level of deprivation, about 6 percent of nonmetro families have income below half their poverty level. This compares to 4 percent in metro places. Taken together, these results confirm that poverty rates are about one-and-a-half times greater in nonmetro than metro America.

Data on annual family income and family earnings also indicate greater economic well-being in metro areas. Mean total family income in metro areas exceeds that of nonmetro areas by 37 percent. The corresponding figure for annual family earnings is 47 percent. While some assert that this income gap is tempered by the greater cost of living in urban areas (Watkins and Watkins 1984), another work casts doubt on any great cost of living difference between metro and nonmetro places (Ghelfi 1987).

Much policy and public attention have been paid to poverty in the inner cities of metro areas. The recent flurry of work on the urban "underclass" (Auletta 1982; Wilson 1987; Ricketts and Sawhill 1985) attests to the persistence of this topic. The data in Table 2.1 justify this concern. By all three measures, poverty is as prevalent in central cities as it is in rural areas. Respectively, 15.2 and 15.4 percent of nonmetro and central city families are poor. The gap is greater when more severe poverty levels are considered. That is, although central city poverty exceeded nonmetro poverty by only about 1 percent in relative terms, the gap was closer to 9 percent when the 75-percent and 50-percent poverty thresholds are used. Still, although central cities do have the highest incidence of poverty, the rates are not appreciably greater than those found in nonmetro areas; and although inner city poverty has garnered the greater popular concern, the absolute number of poor families is about the same in nonmetro America.

Given the higher incidence of poverty in central cities and nonmetro areas, one would expect greater use of welfare there. As seen in Table 2.1, this expectation holds only for central city families, among whom 10.3 percent received welfare income in 1986. (It is noteworthy that this is substantially less than their poverty rate.) Despite the fact that their poverty rate was about the same as central city families, only 5.9 percent of nonmetro families received welfare income. This figure is not significantly different from that of metro families generally (5.8 percent), who have a far lower poverty rate than nonmetro families. Thus, considering their high poverty risks, nonmetro families have a remarkably low rate of welfare receipt, a conclusion that finds support in the next row of Table 2.1. The percent of poor families that received welfare income was considerably greater in metro areas (41.8 percent) and central cities (49.9 percent), than in rural areas (30.2 percent).

Not only do nonmetro families have a comparatively low rate of welfare receipt, among those families that *did* receive welfare, the mean annual welfare income was lowest among nonmetro families (Table 2.1). The mean receipt among nonmetro families ($2,928) is significantly less than that for metro families ($3,652) and for central city families ($3,911).

## Ameliorative Effects: Descriptive Results

Since nonmetro poor families are far less likely than their metro counterparts to receive welfare income, and since the average annual welfare receipt (among recipients) is lower among nonmetro than metro families, it is reasonable to expect that welfare's ameliorative impact on family poverty is less in nonmetro America. The data in Table 2.2 strongly support this hypothesis.

Four measures of amelioration are presented in Table 2.2. In the first, for each family, welfare income is subtracted from total family income. This pre–welfare income is then compared to the absolute poverty threshold. The first ameliorative effect measure is the percent of those families with pre–welfare income below poverty whose total family income is at or above poverty. In other words, among those families that are poor without welfare, what percent are brought above poverty via welfare? As seen in Table 2.2, surprisingly few families enjoy a positive ameliorative effect, so defined. Only about 5 percent of pre–welfare poor families are brought above poverty in metro areas, though somewhat more (5.7 percent) are positively affected in central cities. As expected, however, the ameliorative effect is considerably lower (2.1 percent) in nonmetro America.

The second and third ameliorative effects are variants of the first. The second asks, among those families whose pre–welfare income is less than 75 percent of their absolute poverty threshold, what percent are brought above this cutoff via welfare income? The third measure is the same, but it uses 50

**Table 2.2**
**Nonmetro/Metro Differences in the Ameliorative Effect of**
**Welfare on Poverty**

| Ameliorative Effect Measures | Nonmetro Total | Metro Total | Central City |
|---|---|---|---|
| Percent with pre–welfare income below poverty brought above poverty by welfare | 2.1 | 4.7* | 5.7* |
| Percent with pre–welfare income below .75 of poverty brought above .75 of poverty by welfare | 5.9 | 10.0* | 10.3* |
| Percent with pre–welfare income below .50 of poverty brought above .50 of poverty by welfare | 20.9 | 32.2* | 34.9* |
| Mean proportion of pre–welfare poverty gap that is closed by welfare | 16.5 | 31.7* | 35.9* |

* T-test with respect to nonmetro areas significant at p < .01.

Source: March 1987 Current Population Survey, U.S. Census Bureau.

percent of the absolute poverty threshold. Both the second and third rows of Table 2.2 continue to show that the ameliorative effect of welfare on family poverty is considerably greater in metro areas (central cities in particular) than in nonmetro places. Only 20.9 percent of nonmetro families with pre–welfare income below 50 percent of poverty are brought above this level via welfare. This compares to 32.2 percent in metro areas generally and 34.9 percent in central cities.

These binary measures of welfare's ability to alleviate poverty have some intuitive appeal in view of policy goals—welfare either does or does not lift families out of poverty. A less stark approach is to ask to what degree welfare closes the gap between a family's pre–welfare income and its poverty line.[4] This measure, expressed as a percentage, is referred to herein as closure.

The data on closure (Table 2.2, row 4) indicate again that welfare has a much greater ameliorative effect in metro than nonmetro areas. On the average, less than 17 percent of the pre-welfare poverty gap among non-metro families was closed via welfare benefits; the corresponding figure for metro families was about 32 percent. Closure was even greater among central city families, among whom nearly 36 percent of the pre-welfare poverty gap was closed.

To summarize, at this descriptive level, I have shown that the ameliorative effect of welfare—its ability to reduce poverty—is greater in metro than nonmetro America. Moreover, according to all four measures, the ameliorative effect is stronger in central cities than in metro areas generally. This is so despite the commensurate degree of deprivation in central city and nonmetro places. The balance of this chapter explores the rural-urban differences in ameliorative effects more closely.

## Ameliorative Effects: Multivariate Models

The descriptive analyses have revealed important reasons why welfare does not alleviate poverty as much in rural areas as in urban places. The rural poor are not as likely to receive welfare in the first place, and those who do, do not receive as much on an annual basis as their metro counterparts. A reasonable explanation for the latter is that the nonmetro poor tend to live in states, particularly in the South, that have lower benefit levels.

To quantify these explanations, Table 2.3 presents an ordinary least squares (OLS) regression of the closure variable on three independent variables. The first of these predictors is type of residence, measured as two dummy variables—metro outside central cities and nonmetro. The comparison group is families in central cities. The second independent variable, designed to measure interstate differences in welfare benefits, is the maximum AFDC payment to one needy adult and two children (with no other

**Table 2.3**
**Ordinary Least Squares Regression of Ameliorative Effect of Welfare**
**(standardized coefficients with unstandardized coefficients in parentheses)**

| Independent Variable | Model 1 | Model 2 | Model 3 |
|---|---|---|---|
| Type of Residence | | | |
|   Metro outside central city | −.026 | −.006 | .035* |
| | (−.052) | (−.011) | (.067) |
|   Nonmetro | −.077** | −.041** | .007 |
| | (−.156) | (−.082) | (.014) |
| State AFDC Benefit Level | | .143** | .085** |
| | | (.001) | (.001) |
| Receipt of Welfare | | | .302** |
| | | | (.581) |
| Constant | (.314) | (−.066) | (−.219) |
| $R^2$ | .005 | .024 | .10ს |
| N | 4513 | 4513 | 4513 |

* Significant at $p < .05$.
** Significant at $p < .01$

Source: March 1987 Current Population Survey, U.S. Census Bureau.

income) for the family's state of residence (U.S. Department of Health and Human Services 1987). These payment levels range from \$118 in Alabama to \$740 in Alaska. The final variable predicting closure is simply whether the family received AFDC and/or general assistance in the year prior to the survey. With the exception of type of residence, all variables reference the family's situation in 1986.

Table 2.3 presents three OLS models that were estimated on pre-welfare poor families. The first includes only the type of residence variables. This model confirms that the ameliorative effect of welfare is significantly less in nonmetro areas than it is in central cities. Model 2 includes the family's state benefit level. This variable has a positive effect meaning that families living in states with higher benefit levels enjoy a greater ameliorative effect. That the effect of nonmetro status is attenuated by nearly half (from −0.194 to −0.104), confirms that part of the reason for the smaller ameliorative effect among nonmetro families is that they live in states with lower benefit levels. Even in model 2, however, the ameliorative effect is significantly less in nonmetro places than central cities. To determine the degree to which this might be due to their lower likelihood of receiving welfare, model 3 includes the term indicating whether welfare income was received in the previous year. As expected, this term has a strong and positive effect. More importantly, the effect of nonmetro status becomes insignificant. This indicates that an important reason why welfare alleviates poverty to a smaller degree in nonmetro areas is because the nonmetro poor are less likely to receive it than their metro counterparts. The remainder of this analysis seeks to determine why this is so.

### Determinants of Welfare Receipt among Poor Families

At a theoretical level, many factors could determine whether a given poor family will receive welfare income. One important group of variables describes a family's eligibility for AFDC or general assistance. Obviously, in order to qualify for AFDC, a family has to have dependent children, and in about half the states, the recipient cannot be married with a spouse present. However, simply because a family is eligible for welfare does not mean it will receive it. Some parents may simply be unaware that they are eligible; others may not wish to bear the social stigma attached to welfare receipt (Feagin 1975).

In this section, logistic regression analysis is used to estimate models of welfare receipt among families. This method is appropriate since the dependent variable is binary—either a family did or did not receive welfare income in the year prior to the survey (1986). The intent is to confirm that nonmetro families are significantly less likely to receive welfare income and to explain this difference.

### Definition of Variables and Hypothesized Effects

In the following paragraphs, the independent variables are defined, and their hypothesized effects on the propensity of families to receive welfare are discussed. Type of residence is defined as it was in the OLS models. That is, with the comparison group being families in central cities, two dummy variables identify metro families outside central cities and nonmetro families. I expect the effect of the latter variable to be negative and significant, indicating a lower probability of welfare receipt among nonmetro poor families.

A variable indicating that a family head did not work at all in the previous year is expected to have a positive effect on receipt. Other things equal, families headed by a nonworker will be more likely to turn to welfare as a means of subsistence.

Two binary variables, one indicating the presence of own children under eighteen years of age and the other indicating that the family is headed by a married couple, are used to control for eligibility for AFDC.[5] Empirically, it is difficult to model eligibility with Current Population Survey (CPS) data because the many variables needed are not available and because of vast interstate differences in eligibility criteria. Consideration is given to these two variables—presence of children and family type—because they are important and available and because they may vary systematically between metro and nonmetro areas. It is expected that the presence of children will have a positive effect on receipt and that married couple headship will have a negative effect, other things equal.

Three additional independent variables describe the family head. These are education, race, and age. Education, defined as grades of school completed, has a theoretically ambiguous effect on welfare receipt. The better educated poor could be more likely to receive benefits if they are more cognizant of available programs and how to apply for them. They could be less likely to receive if they are more aware of and more qualified for employment opportunities. The better educated poor may also be more sensitive to mainstream attitudes against welfare receipt. Since AFDC is generally utilized by the young, the age of the family head is expected to have a negative effect.

Finally, three additional situational variables are considered. First, home ownership is expected to have a negative effect on receipt. While not itself an eligibility criterion, it may be related to the ownership of other assets which can compromise eligibility. Second, families that live in states that offer AFDC to unemployed parents (AFDC-UP) are expected to be more likely to receive welfare than those that do not. Third, theoretically, poor families will seek welfare in direct proportion to average benefit levels. Accordingly, I expect state benefit level (maximum benefit payment to one needy adult and two dependent children) to have a positive effect on receipt, ceteris paribus. The correlation matrix for these variables appears in Table 2.4.

### Results

The logistic regression models of welfare receipt are presented in Table 2.5. Model 1 contains only the two dummy variables for type of residence. As expected, compared to central city poor families, nonmetro poor families are significantly less likely to receive welfare income. Metro families outside of inner cities are also less likely to receive than inner city families, but the effect is not as strong.

The OLS models suggested that much of the reason why the ameliorative effect of welfare income was less in nonmetro areas was because the nonmetro poor are less likely to receive it in the first place. With this now confirmed by model 1, it is important to determine why.

The first explanation considered pertains to work commitment. It has been asserted (Watkins and Watkins 1984) and research has shown (Bloomquist, Jensen, and Teixeira 1987) that rural people have a particularly high attachment to the labor force. This is borne out by the negative association

**Table 2.4**
**Matrix of Correlations for Variables Used in Logistic Regression of Welfare Receipt**

| | | (1) | (2) | (3) | (4) | (5) | (6) | (7) | (8) | (9) | (10) | (11) |
|---|---|---|---|---|---|---|---|---|---|---|---|---|
| Welfare Rcpt | (1) | ---- | | | | | | | | | | |
| Met not city | (2) | -.057 | ---- | | | | | | | | | |
| Nonmetro | (3) | -.121 | -.495 | ---- | | | | | | | | |
| Did not work | (4) | .278 | -.061 | -.088 | ---- | | | | | | | |
| Child present | (5) | .288 | .020* | -.074 | -.198 | ---- | | | | | | |
| Married couple | (6) | -.246 | .025 | .093 | -.045 | -.244 | ---- | | | | | |
| Non-white | (7) | .160 | -.148 | -.230 | .115 | .069 | -.152 | ---- | | | | |
| Age | (8) | -.275 | -.033 | .098 | .255 | -.671 | .326 | -.061 | ---- | | | |
| Own home | (9) | -.356 | .051 | .203 | -.025 | -.318 | .245 | -.228 | .430 | ---- | | |
| Education | (10) | -.020* | .065 | -.029 | -.192 | .206 | -.167 | -.200 | -.315 | -.034 | ---- | |
| AFDC-UP state | (11) | .249 | -.024* | -.205 | .096 | .109 | -.047 | -.071 | -.117 | -.143 | .120 | ---- |
| State AFDC pay | (12) | .194 | .035 | -.228 | .051 | .109 | -.051 | -.018* | -.128 | -.172 | .095 | .722 |

* Correlation not significant at p < .05.

Source: March 1987 Current Population Survey, U.S. Census Bureau.

**Table 2.5**
**Logistic Regression of Receipt of Welfare Income among the**
**Pre-Welfare Poor[a]**

| Independent Variable | Model 1 | Model 2 | Model 3 | Model 4 |
|---|---|---|---|---|
| Type of Residence | | | | |
| Metro outside central city | -.316** | -.253** | -.218** | -.045 |
| Nonmetro | -.497** | -.416** | -.314** | .014 |
| Head did not work last year | | .568** | .779** | .759** |
| Own children < 18 present | | | .886** | .568** |
| Married couple head | | | -.441** | -.368** |
| Head is non-white | | | | .089* |
| Head's age | | | | -.010** |
| Family's home is owned | | | | -.533** |
| Head's education | | | | -.036** |
| Family's state offers AFDC-UP | | | | .487** |
| State benefit level | | | | .000 |
| Intercept | 5.050 | 4.704 | 3.994 | 4.685 |
| N | 5,013 | 5,013 | 5,013 | 5,013 |

[a] Cell entries are SPSS-X logistic regression coefficients.

* Significant at $p < .05$.
** Significant at $p < .01$

Source: March 1987 Current Population Survey, U.S. Census Bureau.

$(-0.088)$ between nonmetro residence and having a family head who did not work in the previous year (see Table 2.4). Having a working head can reduce the propensity to receive public assistance because it reduces eligibility and may reflect a stronger commitment to work over welfare, other things equal. Conversely, if a head does not work, the family is left with fewer alternatives to transfer programs. The coefficient for having a non-working head is strong and positive; these families are more likely to receive welfare. More importantly, the effect of nonmetro residence is attenuated, suggesting that part of the reason why the nonmetro poor are less likely to receive welfare than their central city counterparts is because they are more likely to have a working head. The same can be said for metro residents outside central cities.

In model 3, two additional independent variables are added. As noted above, the presence of own children and being a two-parent family can greatly affect eligibility for AFDC. Both variables behave as expected, and the effect of nonmetro residence is further attenuated. As indicated by the correlations in Table 2.4, nonmetro families are slightly less apt to have own children and more likely to be headed by a married couple. Both of these factors work to reduce welfare receipt among nonmetro families.

Six additional variables are entered in the final model (model 4). The bivariate relationships reveal that four of these variables further explain the lower welfare receipt among nonmetro famlies: 1) nonmetro families are less likely to be headed by a nonwhite, and nonwhites are more likely to receive welfare; 2) nonmetro family heads tend to be older, and older heads are less likely to receive; 3) nonmetro poor families are more likely to own their home, and home ownership lowers receipt; and 4) nonmetro poor families are less likely to live in states with AFDC-UP, and the latter increases the likelihood of welfare receipt. As a result, the negative direct effect of nonmetro residence on receipt is completely explained.

Separate models (not shown) indicate that among the final variables entered, home ownership and AFDC-UP play the greatest role in explaining away the nonmetro effect. That home ownership should have such a strong effect is intriguing, since federal requirements exclude the value of homes from eligibility criteria in all states (U.S. Department of Health and Human Services 1987). It may, however, be related to the ownership of other assets that do cause ineligibility. Home ownership may also indicate greater economic well-being among these otherwise poor families and less need for welfare. Finally, some might not apply for welfare benefits because they assume (erroneously) that home ownership renders them ineligible, and that the only way they can receive benefits is to sell their home.

That AFDC-UP should increase receipt is also interesting considering that the marital status of family head is controlled. It is plausible, however, that states with AFDC-UP have more liberal eligibility criteria in other ways as well. These states may also have less of a negative stigma attached to welfare receipt. It is noteworthy that, by and large, states without AFDC-UP are clustered in the South and Southwest of the United States. These states tend to offer lower welfare benefits (Levitan 1985) and have stricter eligibility criteria in general (U.S. Department of Health and Human Services 1987).

## SUMMARY AND CONCLUSIONS

The purpose of this chapter was to refocus attention on the degree to which welfare alleviates poverty by highlighting and explaining rural-urban differences in this ameliorative effect. The discussion opened with descriptive tables, which revealed considerably greater poverty and lower incomes in nonmetro as compared to metro areas. Despite this, the rate of welfare receipt was not appreciably higher in the countryside, and mean welfare receipt among recipients was considerably lower there.

The resurgence of interest in an urban underclass has once again placed urban poverty at the forefront of national attention (Wilson 1987). The data in Table 2.1 justified this concern, but central city poverty rates were not appreciably greater than those of nonmetro families. Consistent with the underclass notion, inner city families were far more likely to receive welfare, and the recipients received considerably higher total benefits than their counterparts in nonmetro areas.

Considering their comparatively light use of welfare despite a high poverty rate, it is of little surprise that the ameliorative effect of welfare—the degree to which it reduces poverty—was much lower among nonmetro poor families (Table 2.2). This finding was consistent across four different measures of amelioration.

A key reason for the lesser ameliorative effect among nonmetro poor families was their lower propensity to receive any benefits at all. Nonmetro poor families were less likely to receive welfare than their central city counterparts because, on average, they are (1) more likely to have a working family head, (2) less likely to have own children present, (3) more likely to be headed by a married couple, (4) less likely to be headed by a nonwhite, (5) more likely to have older heads, (6) more likely to own their home, and (7) less likely to live in a state that offers AFDC-UP.

These findings have implications for recent attempts at welfare reform. At this writing, the Family Welfare Reform Act of 1987 (H.R. 1720) has passed the House and awaits Senate debate. As noted above the bill stresses remedial training and job placement services. Many able-bodied welfare recipients would be required to at least look for work, if not hold a job, or face loss or reduction of benefits (Knudsen 1987). This bill is the result of the mounting concern over welfare dependency. I have argued that this concern arises largely from observations of inner city poverty and scholarly work on the urban underclass. If enacted, however, the new welfare system will also be serving the rural poor. If the thrust of the reform is to instill a greater work ethic and more stable family environment then it is less relevant in nonmetro areas. I have shown that nonmetro poor families are more likely to have working heads and be headed by a married couple. One aspect of the bill that would disproportionately benefit the nonmetro poor is the nationalization of the AFDC-UP program. Since the nonmetro poor are relatively overrepresented in states without AFDC-UP and since they are more likely to be married, they should be helped significantly by this provision.

While welfare accounts for the majority of all public assistance recipients (Levitan 1985), another important component of public assistance is Supplemental Security Income (SSI), which provides cash support for the poor who are aged, blind, or disabled. Auxiliary analyses[6] of rural-urban differences in the utilization and ameliorative effects of SSI revealed that, contrary to the pattern for welfare receipt, rural poor families and individuals were significantly *more* likely to receive SSI than their counterparts in metro areas. This partly reflects the comparatively large number of aged people in rural compared to urban areas. However, like the welfare results, nonmetro SSI recipients received significantly less cash from this program, on average, than did metro SSI recipients. These countervailing influences resulted in little rural-urban difference in the ability of SSI to reduce poverty.

## NOTES

1. In this chapter I use the terms urban and metro, and rural and nonmetro interchangeably. In the data analysis, however, the key empirical distinction is between metro and nonmetro areas.

2. Another important component of the public safety net is Supplemental Security Income (SSI), which is aimed toward the aged, blind, and disabled poor. I chose not to include SSI in this analysis since it is meant for the so-called "deserving" poor, and thus is not central to current debates over welfare policy. Moreover, being a nationalized program, SSI is not as plagued by geographic variation in eligibility criteria and program benefits. Nevertheless, I carried out auxiliary analyses of rural-urban differences in the utilization and ameliorative effects of SSI and briefly discuss these results in the concluding section.

3. Here I use the official definition of absolute poverty (U.S. Census Bureau 1987), whereby a family is poor if their total annual income is less than the amount needed to provide a minimum standard of living.

4. Among families in poverty, the difference between their total income and the poverty threshold is frequently referred to as the poverty gap.

5. That a family is headed by a married couple does not necessarily mean it will be ineligible for AFDC. Some states offer AFDC to married couples if one or both of the parents are unemployed (AFDC-UP). Also, it is possible for a married couple to have an unwed daughter with a dependent child and for the daughter to receive AFDC.

The latter circumstance points to an analytic problem that deserves mention. My unit of analysis is the census family, which is defined as all people living together who are related by blood, marriage, or adoption. This family unit is more inclusive than the family definition used by AFDC. To determine eligibility, AFDC looks only at the characteristics of the prospective AFDC parent and his or her dependent children. I use family head variables to monitor eligibility. To the extent that AFDC parents are not the family heads, my methodology mismeasures certain eligibility criteria. This problem is less relevant for the aggregate ameliorative effect measures than it is for the multivariate analyses of welfare receipt.

6. Tables accompanying these auxiliary analyses are available upon request from the author.

## REFERENCES

Bloomquist, Leonard E., Leif Jensen, and Ruy A. Teixeira. 1987. " 'Workfare' and

Nonmetropolitan America: An Assessment of the Employment Opportunities for Nonmetro Welfare Clients." Paper presented at the Ninth Annual Research Conference of the Association for Public Policy Analysis and Management, Bethesda, Md., October 29-31.

Carlson, John E., Marie L. Lassey, and William R. Lassey. 1981. *Rural Society and Environment in America.* New York: McGraw-Hill.

Deavers, Kenneth L., Robert A. Hoppe, and Peggy J. Ross. 1986. "Public Policy and Rural Poverty: A View from the 1980s." *Policy Studies Journal* 51(2): 291-309.

Feagin, Joe R. 1975. *Subordinating the Poor: Welfare and American Beliefs.* Englewood Cliffs, N.J.: Prentice-Hall.

Ghelfi, Linda M. 1987. "Income, Needs and Expenditures: Metro-Nonmetro Differences in Wisconsin." Paper presented at the 50th annual meeting of the Rural Sociological Society, Madison, Wisconsin, August 13-15.

Hopkins, Kevin R. 1987. *Welfare Dependency: Behavior, Culture, and Public Policy.* U.S. Department of Health and Human Services, OS, ASPE. Washington, D.C.: U.S. Government Printing Office.

Hoppe, Robert A. 1980. "Despite Progress, Rural Poverty Demands Attention." *Rural Development Perspectives* (March): 7-10.

Institute for Research on Poverty, University of Wisconsin, Madison. 1980. "On Not Reaching the Rural Poor: Urban Bias in Poverty Policy." *Focus* 4(2): 5-8.

Jensen, Leif. 1987. "Rural Minority Families in the United States: A Twenty-Year Profile of Poverty and Economic Well-Being." Paper presented at the 50th annual meeting of the Rural Sociological Society, Madison, Wisconsin, August 13-15.

Knudsen, Patrick L. 1987. "After Long, Bruising Battle, House Approves Welfare Bill." *Congressional Quarterly* (December 19): 3157-65.

Levitan, Sar A. 1985. *Programs in Aid of the Poor.* 5th ed. Baltimore, Md.: The Johns Hopkins University Press.

Murray, Charles. 1984. *Losing Ground: American Social Policy, 1950-1980.* New York: Basic Books.

Ricketts, Erol R., and Isabel V. Sawhill. 1985. "Defining and Measuring the Underclass." *Journal of Policy Analysis and Management* 7(2): 316-25.

Rodgers, Harrell R., Jr., and Gregory R. Weiher. 1986. "The Rural Poor in America: A Statistical Overview." *Policy Studies Journal* 15(2): 279-90.

Schiller, Bradley R. 1980. *The Economics of Poverty and Discrimination.* 3d ed. Englewood Cliffs, N.J.: Prentice-Hall.

U.S. Bureau of the Census. 1987. "Money Income and Poverty Status of Families and Persons in the United States: 1986." Current Population Reports, Series P-60, no. 157 (Advance data from the March 1987 Current Population Survey.) Washington, D.C.: U.S. Government Printing Office.

U.S. Department of Health and Human Services. 1987. *Characteristics of State Plans for Aid to Families with Dependent Children.* Washington, D.C.: U.S. Government Printing Office.

Watkins, Julia M., and Dennis A. Watkins. 1984. *Social Policy and the Rural Setting.* New York: Springer.

Wilson, William Julius. 1987. *The Truly Disadvantaged: The Inner City, the Underclass, and Public Policy.* Chicago: University of Chicago Press.

## 3
# Labor Force Participation and Poverty Status among Rural and Urban Women Who Head Families

ELEANOR CAUTLEY and DORIS P. SLESINGER

## INTRODUCTION

Two trends in the United States are absorbing the interest of researchers: one is the increasing proportion of women in the poor population, often termed the feminization of poverty; the other is the increasing proportion of women who have entered the labor force. This chapter examines one group in which these two trends meet: women without husbands who head family households. Women who head families, along with their children, are among the poorest groups in the United States, yet a large proportion of these women are working. This analysis focuses on the associations between work and poverty, mediated by other conditions, for these "single mothers." We suggest that the relationship between work and poverty differs between urban and rural areas, depending on both the individual characteristics of the women and the economic characteristics of their residential areas.

The first trend, the increasing proportion of mothers within the poor population, has recently been documented by Irwin Garfinkel and Sara McLanahan (1985), using national data from 1967 through 1983. They demonstrate that the feminization of poverty is due both to the rapid increase in the proportion of families headed by women and to the decreasing poverty among other groups, especially the elderly. They note that the proportion of the poor represented by women with children has increased every year until 1978, when it started to decline. Garfinkel and McLanahan (1986) also indicate three factors that lead to greater poverty for single mothers and their children: (1) low earnings capacity for women in the labor market, (2) low or nonexistent income contributions from the absent father, and (3) low amounts received from public assistance programs. The first, low earnings capacity, is not a new phenomenon for women. When coupled with responsibility for supporting a family, it not infrequently means poverty for that family. Lack of monetary contribution from absent fathers is still in evidence today, although some states are starting to garnishee fathers' wages. Finally, Aid to Families with Dependent Children (AFDC) payments are usually near or below poverty level for the family.

The trend of increasing female participation in the labor force was noted in the mid-1960s by Valerie K. Oppenheimer (1970) and more recently by others (Taeuber and Valdisera 1986; Bianchi and Spain 1986; O'Connell and Bloom 1987). By 1980, 50 percent of women aged sixteen and older were in the labor force. Women's participation in the labor force is not automatically associated with reduction or elimination of poverty, although it may reduce poverty among married women in two-earner families. An additional factor is segmentation of the labor market by gender (Waite 1981). Women tend to work in female-dominated occupations, which have lower pay scales than male-dominated occupations. And there is evidence that women, especially those with children, are less likely to work full-time than men (Taeuber and Valdisera 1986). All of these factors make for an interesting and complex set of relationships between working and poverty.

Previous research that examined rural/urban differences utilized the census classification of metropolitian/nonmetropolitan areas. This classification is based on county lines. Using this geographic classification can lead to inaccurate labelling of "rural/urban" areas. For example, some metropolitan counties that contain a place of 50,000 or more also contain low density or rural areas. Other counties contain medium size cities (under 50,000) and are classified as "nonmetropolitan," although they are adjacent to large urban centers. The analysis presented here is based on another census classification, the concept of "Urbanized Area" (UA). This does not use county lines, but rather the boundaries of incorporated places that are located adjacent to or near cities of 50,000 or more.

The following designations are used in this analysis, based on the level of "urbanization."[1]

| | |
|---|---|
| CENTRAL CITY | In urbanized area, the central city |
| SUBURB | In urbanized area, but outside the central city |
| SMALL TOWN | Outside urbanized area, but in place of 2,500 or more inhabitants |
| RURAL | Remaining area outside urbanized area |

We now turn to an examination of these residential areas, looking at single mothers' labor force participation and poverty status in urban and rural areas. We will examine characteristics of the women living in these areas, such as age, age of children, marital status, race, and education. Finally, we will compare the results of multivariate analyses of poverty among women who live in four residential areas: central cities, suburbs, small towns, and rural areas.

## DATA SOURCE

The data utilized for this analysis consist of a stratified random sample of female householders with dependent children drawn from the 1980 Public Use Microdata Sample of the U.S. Census. The sample was stratified by urban/rural residence in order to obtain sufficient cases for the rural analysis. Ten percent of urban and 20 percent of rural households with a female householder were randomly selected, and only those containing children under the age of eighteen of the householder were included in this analysis.[2]

Thus, the 5,796 households sampled for this research are female-headed family households with one or more own children of the head under age eighteen. They are a representative sample of the 4.9 million such households in the United States in 1980. The sampled households range in size from two to fifteen persons; 90 percent have from two to five persons. The characteristics of the head—always a woman—are of primary interest here.

## CHARACTERISTICS OF FEMALE FAMILY HEADS

The age of the family head ranges from sixteen to eighty-four, with four-fifths between the ages of twenty and forty-four. Since all of these women, even the elderly, have a child of their own under age eighteen, we assume that some of these children are adopted or are stepchildren. Some of the adopted children are presumably grandchildren of the head, who have come into her care through a variety of circumstances. Two-thirds of the women have only school-age children (ages six to seventeen); the remainder have one or more preschoolers.

Almost half of the female heads are divorced, another 21 percent are separated, 17 percent are single, and 12 percent are widowed. The remaining 4 percent are married, spouse absent. This latter group includes both women who live apart from their husbands through choice or necessity, such as some wives of servicemen, and women who have been deserted but do not consider themselves to be separated. Over four-fifths of all women in this sample have been married at some time.

About 62 percent of the female heads are white, about 32 percent are black, and another 6 percent are of other nonwhite races.

About 66 percent of these women have a high school diploma or more education. Only 12 percent have less than a ninth grade education.

Over two-thirds of the female heads worked during 1979. The majority of these worked full-time, as measured by 1,750 or more total hours worked during the year.[3]

The households in this sample are classified into four groups, according to area of residence. The four areas and the distribution of the 4.9 million single-mother households in the United States as well as this sample in 1980 are as follows: central city (44 percent), suburb (29 percent), small town (12 percent), and rural (15 percent). The distribution of *all* U.S. family households with minor children, however, is markedly different: central cities contain 27 percent of all such families, suburbs 33 percent, small towns 12 percent, and rural areas 28 percent. Thus, single-mother families are much more likely to live in central cities than are other families and, conversely, much less likely to live in rural areas.

The characteristics of these women vary across the four residential types (see Table 3.1). Central city women tend to be younger than the average while rural women are somewhat older. It follows that the central city women have a larger proportion of young children than the other groups, while the children of rural women tend to be older.

About half of the women in the suburbs, small towns, and rural areas are divorced. The proportion divorced is lower in the central cities, which has higher proportions of single and separated women. The proportion of widowed women is much higher in the rural area than elsewhere, corresponding again to the older mean age in rural areas.

Women of color are much more likely to live in central cities than elsewhere. Previous research has demonstrated that black mothers are more likely to be unmarried than are white mothers (Garfinkel and McLanahan 1986). This association may account for the larger proportion of single women in the central city area. This will be explored further in the multivariate analysis below.

Educational attainment also varies by area of residence; central city and rural women are less likely to have completed high school than others; suburban women have the highest attainment levels overall.

The work status distribution for 1979 also differs by residential area. Central city women are least likely, and suburban women are most likely, to have worked in 1979. The proportions who worked full-time have less variation, but the pattern is similar; the largest proportion of full-time workers is among suburban women. Over one-third of central city women did not work during 1979; the proportion of nonworkers for each of the remaining three groups is closer to one-fourth.

## POVERTY STATUS

Single mothers with their children are disproportionately represented in the poverty population. Overall, 42 percent of this sample of women with dependent children is poor. The poverty measure used is the standard

Census one, based on 1979 family income and family size. All cases falling below the 100-percent threshold are labeled "poor" in this analysis. Table 3.2 presents the proportion of poor among the sampled women, based on their characteristics. Among the areas of residence, central city women are most likely to be poor, followed by small town and rural women, while suburban women are least likely to be poor. Although not presented in the table, it is noteworthy that all of these poverty rates are two or three times higher than comparable rates for all families with related children under age eighteen.

Younger women (under age thirty) and women with young children are more prone to poverty than the older groups. Indeed, younger women living in suburban areas are twice as likely to be poor as their older counterparts. Differences between younger and older women are strong in all residential areas. Women age fifty and older are the least poor, except for those living in small towns.

Poverty in the various marital status groups seems to represent two different situations. Poverty rates for divorced and widowed women are much lower—almost half—than those for single, separated, and married women. This may be because the relationship between the family's financial status and the absent father has been formalized in cases of divorce and widowhood; many divorced fathers have court orders to pay child support. Widowed mothers gain access to social security (old age and survivors benefits) and other post-employment benefits. In the case of some single, separated, and married mothers, the father may rarely, if ever, contribute to the family's income.

Poverty rates are much higher for nonwhite than for white women in all residential areas. Women who have not graduated from high school are more likely to be poor than are more educated women.

The poverty rate for women who did not work in 1979 is three times as high as the rate of women who worked. This is not at all surprising since wages provide a major portion of the income for all persons in this population. In addition, a self-selection process occurs whereby those with more education are likely to have marketable skills, and thus are more likely to be working than those who have few skills. Women who worked 1,750 hours or more during 1979 (i.e., full-time workers) are much less likely to be poor than are women who worked part-time.

Again, there are distinct differences in the poverty rates among the four areas of residence. By far, the highest poverty rate in this sample occurs among central city women who did not work in 1979—82.5 percent were poor. Because the proportion of women not working in central cities is much higher than in any other area and because the central city group is very large, this poverty rate most probably accounts for their higher overall poverty rate of almost 48 percent.

However, the poverty rates of small town women rank higher than central city women for a number of characteristics. Women who are sepa-

Table 3.1
Characteristics of Female-Headed Family Households by Urban/Rural Residence, 1980

| Characteristics | Urban Central City | Urban Suburb | Small Town | Rural | Total Number | Total Percent |
|---|---|---|---|---|---|---|
| **Age** | | | | | | |
| 16-19 | 1.5% | 1.0% | 1.0% | 0.7% | 68 | 1.2% |
| 20-29 | 31.9 | 24.9 | 30.1 | 23.7 | 1,645 | 28.4 |
| 30-39 | 40.1 | 42.6 | 36.3 | 38.6 | 2,325 | 40.1 |
| 40-49 | 18.7 | 22.2 | 23.2 | 25.2 | 1,231 | 21.2 |
| 50-59 | 7.1 | 8.5 | 7.8 | 10.7 | 473 | 8.2 |
| 60+ | 0.7 | 0.8 | 1.6 | 1.1 | 53 | 0.9 |
| | | | | | | |
| Mean Age | 34.4 | 35.8 | 35.6 | 37.0 | | 35.3 |
| | | | | | | |
| **Own Children** | | | | | | |
| Some <6 years | 39.4 | 31.7 | 33.7 | 29.0 | 2,022 | 34.9 |
| Age 6-17 only | 60.6 | 68.3 | 66.3 | 71.0 | 3,773 | 65.1 |
| | | | | | | |
| **Marital Status** | | | | | | |
| Ever Married | 75.6 | 87.8 | 88.5 | 90.4 | 4,810 | 83.0 |
| Married | 3.7 | 2.9 | 5.5 | 3.9 | 215 | 3.7 |
| Divorced | 38.6 | 54.9 | 50.7 | 49.0 | 2,689 | 46.4 |
| Separated | 24.1 | 19.5 | 18.3 | 16.7 | 1,214 | 20.9 |
| Widowed | 9.2 | 10.6 | 13.9 | 20.7 | 692 | 11.9 |
| Single | 24.4 | 12.2 | 11.5 | 9.6 | 986 | 17.0 |

Table 3.1 (continued)

| | Urban | | | | Total | |
| Characteristics | Central City | Suburb | Small Town | Rural | Number | Percent |
|---|---|---|---|---|---|---|
| Race | | | | | | |
| White | 42.8 | 76.1 | 73.6 | 79.5 | 3,581 | 61.8 |
| Black | 49.2 | 19.3 | 22.2 | 15.9 | 1,863 | 32.2 |
| Other | 8.0 | 4.6 | 4.2 | 4.6 | 351 | 6.0 |
| Education Completed | | | | | | |
| 0-8 years | 12.6 | 7.9 | 15.2 | 16.2 | 702 | 12.1 |
| 9-11 years | 25.9 | 17.3 | 23.3 | 22.3 | 1,307 | 22.6 |
| 12 years | 39.0 | 46.9 | 40.8 | 42.7 | 2,439 | 42.1 |
| 13+ years | 22.5 | 27.9 | 20.7 | 18.8 | 1,348 | 23.3 |
| Work in 1979 | | | | | | |
| Yes | 63.6 | 76.7 | 72.9 | 71.7 | 4,044 | 69.8 |
| 1-1749 hours | 27.2 | 30.3 | 30.6 | 31.3 | 1,688 | 29.1 |
| 1750+ hours | 36.5 | 46.4 | 42.3 | 40.4 | 2,356 | 40.6 |
| No | 36.4 | 23.3 | 27.1 | 28.3 | 1,752 | 30.2 |
| N (weighted) | 2,523 | 1,672 | 721 | 879 | 5,796 | |
| Percent | 43.5 | 28.9 | 12.4 | 15.2 | | 100.0 |

Table 3.2
**Proportion in Poverty\* for Selected Characteristics of Female Family Heads with Minor Children by Urban/Rural Residence, 1980**

| Characteristics | Urban | | Small Town | Rural | Total |
|---|---|---|---|---|---|
| | Central City | Suburb | | | |
| Total Proportion Poor | 47.6% | 32.8% | 44.6% | 41.2% | 42.0% |
| **Age** | | | | | |
| <30 | 59.8 | 51.9 | 62.0 | 54.5 | 57.4 |
| 30-49 | 42.0 | 26.5 | 34.6 | 37.0 | 35.6 |
| 50+ | 37.1 | 24.1 | 50.0 | 36.5 | 34.9 |
| **Own Children** | | | | | |
| Some <6 years | 62.7 | 52.9 | 62.0 | 59.5 | 59.6 |
| Age 6-17 only | 37.7 | 23.5 | 35.7 | 33.7 | 32.5 |
| **Marital Status** | | | | | |
| Ever Married | 41.9 | 29.9 | 41.4 | 38.9 | 37.7 |
| Married | 63.3 | 52.4 | 50.0 | 67.2 | 59.0 |
| Divorced | 31.7 | 22.4 | 32.3 | 33.3 | 28.9 |
| Separated | 58.7 | 49.8 | 62.8 | 58.7 | 56.8 |
| Widowed | 32.7 | 25.8 | 43.0 | 30.8 | 31.9 |
| Single | 65.0 | 54.0 | 69.0 | 62.8 | 62.9 |

**Table 3.2** (continued)

| Characteristics | Urban | | Small Town | Rural | Total |
|---|---|---|---|---|---|
| | Central City | Suburb | | | |
| Race | | | | | |
| White | 37.6 | 28.7 | 38.8 | 35.9 | 34.3 |
| Black | 53.5 | 45.3 | 59.9 | 63.2 | 53.3 |
| Other | 64.4 | 48.5 | 65.4 | 56.5 | 60.1 |
| Education | | | | | |
| 0-11 years | 67.5 | 53.7 | 66.0 | 53.8 | 62.1 |
| 12 years | 40.8 | 28.5 | 38.5 | 36.0 | 35.8 |
| 13+ years | 25.2 | 21.3 | 16.5 | 27.2 | 23.1 |
| Work in 1979 | | | | | |
| Yes | 27.6 | 21.7 | 32.7 | 28.3 | 26.5 |
| 1-1749 hours | 48.2 | 45.3 | 59.8 | 47.3 | 48.7 |
| 1750+ hours | 12.2 | 6.3 | 13.0 | 13.5 | 10.6 |
| No | 82.5 | 69.5 | 76.5 | 73.9 | 77.8 |
| Number | 2,523 | 1,672 | 721 | 879 | 5,796 |

* Less than 100% of poverty threshold for 1979 family income.

49

rated, widowed, or single have higher poverty rates than women in other areas. In addition, part-time working women in small towns have higher poverty rates than others.

The rural areas rank third in overall poverty rate. In general, this is also true for the various characteristics listed in Table 3.2. The exceptions occur in marital status, where rural divorced and married women have the highest poverty rates of all four areas, and among rural black and rural college-educated women, who also have the highest poverty rates. Rural women who work full-time have the highest poverty rates of full-time workers.

Almost without exception, the lowest poverty rates occur in the suburbs. Suburban women who worked 1,750 hours or more were actually better off than the national average, with a poverty rate of 6.3 percent. This should not minimize the overall picture; one-third of all suburban female family heads live in poverty.

To recapitulate, poverty rates are much lower among women who worked in 1979, especially among those who worked full-time, than among those who did not work. The variations among areas of residence will be further examined in the next section.

## LABOR FORCE PARTICIPATION AND OCCUPATION

Overall, as shown in Table 3.1, 70 percent of all the female family heads worked during 1979, and 30 percent did not. Among those who worked, the total hours worked during the year (as estimated by weeks worked multiplied by average hours per week) varied considerably. The Bureau of the Census defines full-time as working thirty-five or more hours per week for fifty or more weeks. We convert this to working 1,750 or more hours per year. By this measure, 41 percent of the women in the sample worked full-time during 1979. Part-time workers, those with less than 1,750 work hours, represent 29 percent of the total group. The remaining 30 percent did not work during 1979.

Table 3.3 presents the characteristics of these three groups: nonworkers, part-time workers, and full-time workers. In general, women who did not work, compared to those who did, tended to be at both the young and old ends of the age spectrum, were mothers of preschoolers, and were more likely to be single, widowed, or separated. They also were more likely to be nonwhite, did not complete high school, and were poor. The full-time workers, in contrast, are more likely to be from thirty to forty-nine years old, with school age children, and to be divorced, white, high school graduates, and suburban residents. Characteristics of women working part-time often fell between the nonworkers and the full-time workers. This is especially true when we look at the poverty status; nonworkers are much more likely to be poor than part-time workers, and part-time workers have much higher poverty rates than full-time workers.

We now turn to an examination of the relationship between full-time work and residential area (see Table 3.4). As noted earlier, full-time workers, overall, are more likely to be in the thirty-to-forty-nine-year-old age group; within this group the suburban and small town residents are more likely to be full-time workers. The patterns are different for younger and older workers; among workers under age thirty, rural women are more likely to work full-time; among workers fifty and older, suburban women exhibit the highest proportion working full-time.

In general, suburban workers are most likely to be employed full-time, no matter what characteristic is examined. Suburban women who are age thirty and older, have children of any age, are divorced or single, are white or black, and who have up to twelve years of education are more likely to be working full-time than any other residential group. In fact, suburban women are ranked first or second, in terms of likelihood of being employed full-time, for all but two of the characteristics listed in Table 3.4. The exceptions are in the groups of married and widowed women.

Overall, small town women are next most likely to be working full-time. Small town women who are married with spouse absent, or who have had some college education are more likely to work full-time than women in other areas.

Rural women are next most likely to work full-time. Rural women are more likely to work full-time than any other group when they are under age thirty, have preschool children, are separated, and are in the "other" race groups.

Central city women are the least likely to work full-time, and this pattern holds for many individual characteristics as well. One exception occurs with widows in central cities, who are the most likely of all widows to be working full-time.

Next, we examine the occupational distribution patterns as related to full- or part-time work. Among all women who worked in 1979, those employed in executive, technical, and administrative support occupations are more likely to work full-time; women in sales, service, and farming occupations are more likely to be part-time workers. To some degree, these associations help us understand the residential variations in full-time work. For example, suburban women are more likely to work full-time and are more likely to be employed in the executive and administrative support fields (see Table 3.5). Rural women are more likely to be operators and laborers and in farming, forestry, and fishing, and they are most likely to work part-time. However, a larger proportion of small town women work full-time than do central city and rural women, but small town women are not overrepresented in occupational groups that are more likely to contain full-time workers.

To get a better understanding of the income earned by working mothers in urban and rural areas, we examined the average earnings within each occupational group. To avoid the interpretation problems associated with part-time work, we used a subsample of all women employed full-time in

Table 3.3
**Work Status of Female Family Heads with Minor Children by Selected Characteristics, 1979**

| Characteristics | Did Not Work | Worked Part Time* | Worked Full Time* |
|---|---|---|---|
| Total | 30.2% | 29.1% | 40.7% |
| Age | | | |
| <30 | 34.9 | 34.8 | 30.3 |
| 30-49 | 25.9 | 26.7 | 47.4 |
| 50+ | 44.4 | 26.9 | 28.7 |
| Own Children | | | |
| Some <6 years | 40.2 | 33.1 | 26.7 |
| Age 6-17 only | 24.9 | 27.0 | 48.1 |
| Marital Status | | | |
| Ever Married | 27.8 | 28.8 | 43.4 |
| Married | 38.6 | 33.7 | 27.7 |
| Divorced | 17.6 | 27.6 | 54.8 |
| Separated | 39.0 | 30.2 | 30.8 |
| Widowed | 44.5 | 29.7 | 25.8 |
| Single | 42.0 | 30.5 | 27.5 |

**Table 3.3** (continued)

| Characteristics | Did Not Work | Worked Part Time* | Worked Full Time* |
|---|---|---|---|
| Race | | | |
| White | 24.6 | 30.5 | 44.9 |
| Black | 38.6 | 26.1 | 35.3 |
| Other | 43.6 | 31.6 | 24.8 |
| Education | | | |
| 0-11 years | 48.7 | 28.2 | 23.1 |
| 12 years | 23.7 | 27.8 | 48.5 |
| 13+ years | 14.4 | 33.0 | 52.6 |
| Poverty Status | | | |
| <100% | 56.0 | 33.8 | 10.2 |
| 100+% | 11.6 | 25.8 | 62.6 |
| Residence | | | |
| Central City | 36.4 | 27.2 | 36.4 |
| Suburb | 23.3 | 30.3 | 46.4 |
| Small Town | 27.1 | 30.6 | 42.3 |
| Rural | 28.3 | 31.3 | 40.4 |
| Number | 1,752 | 1,688 | 2,356 |

*Part time work is defined as 1-1,749 hours per year and full time work as 1,750 hours or more.

53

Table 3.4

**Proportion Working Full-Time\* by Selected Characteristics of Female Family Heads with Minor Children by Urban/Rural Residence, 1980**

| Characteristics | Urban | | | Rural | Total |
|---|---|---|---|---|---|
| | Central City | Suburb | Small Town | | |
| Total Working Full Time | 36.5% | 46.4% | 42.3% | 40.4% | 40.6% |
| **Age** | | | | | |
| <30 | 27.0 | 33.0 | 32.3 | 35.7 | 30.3 |
| 30-49 | 42.4 | 53.2 | 51.8 | 45.9 | 47.4 |
| 50+ | 31.8 | 36.1 | 15.5 | 20.2 | 28.7 |
| **Own Children** | | | | | |
| Some <6 years | 23.8 | 29.5 | 29.3 | 29.5 | 26.7 |
| Age 6-17 only | 44.7 | 54.2 | 48.9 | 44.9 | 48.1 |
| **Marital Status** | | | | | |
| Ever Married | 40.4 | 48.1 | 43.6 | 41.5 | 43.4 |
| Married | 22.8 | 26.2 | 41.2 | 27.6 | 27.7 |
| Divorced | 52.4 | 59.1 | 52.1 | 53.4 | 54.8 |
| Separated | 28.0 | 33.3 | 32.7 | 34.9 | 30.8 |
| Widowed | 29.1 | 24.5 | 27.9 | 21.5 | 25.8 |
| Single | 24.3 | 33.9 | 32.4 | 29.7 | 27.4 |

Table 3.4 (continued)

| Characteristics | Urban | | | Rural | Total |
|---|---|---|---|---|---|
| | Central City | Suburb | Small Town | | |
| Race | | | | | |
| White | 42.9 | 47.9 | 45.2 | 42.5 | 45.0 |
| Black | 33.1 | 45.3 | 36.5 | 31.8 | 35.4 |
| Other | 23.0 | 25.8 | 23.1 | 33.3 | 24.8 |
| Education | | | | | |
| 0-11 years | 18.3 | 28.8 | 26.5 | 26.7 | 23.1 |
| 12 years | 45.6 | 51.7 | 49.6 | 49.1 | 48.6 |
| 13+ years | 51.8 | 53.4 | 57.5 | 48.8 | 52.6 |
| Poverty | | | | | |
| <100% | 9.3 | 8.9 | 12.4 | 13.2 | 10.2 |
| 100+% | 61.0 | 64.7 | 66.4 | 59.4 | 62.7 |
| Total Number | 2,523 | 1,672 | 721 | 879 | 5,976 |
| Number Working Full Time | 920 | 776 | 305 | 355 | 2,356 |

*Full time defined as working 1,750 or more hours during 1979.

55

**Table 3.5**

**Occupational Distribution of Employed Female Family Heads with Minor Children by Urban/Rural Residence, 1979**

| Characteristics | Urban | | Small Town | Rural | Total | |
|---|---|---|---|---|---|---|
| | Central City | Suburb | | | Number | Percent |
| Executive, Managerial | 5.7% | 8.3% | 5.6% | 5.5% | 262 | 6.5% |
| Professional | 10.2 | 11.9 | 7.1 | 8.1 | 404 | 10.0 |
| Technical | 3.1 | 3.6 | 3.1 | 2.5 | 127 | 3.1 |
| Sales | 7.6 | 8.9 | 7.6 | 8.1 | 327 | 8.1 |
| Administrative Support | 30.2 | 34.2 | 23.3 | 22.9 | 1,190 | 29.4 |
| Service | 25.9 | 17.3 | 28.7 | 22.4 | 930 | 23.0 |
| Farming, Forestry, Fishing | 0.4 | 0.2 | 0.9 | 3.1 | 33 | 0.8 |
| Precision, Craft | 2.4 | 2.6 | 3.3 | 3.8 | 113 | 2.8 |
| Operators, Laborers | 14.5 | 12.8 | 19.8 | 23.4 | 648 | 16.0 |
| Unknown | – | 0.4 | 0.7 | 0.3 | 10 | 0.2 |
| Number | 1,606 | 1,282 | 526 | 630 | 4,044 | 100.0 |

1979 (2,072 cases). The overall mean earnings in 1979 for these full-time workers was $10,807. There are differences among the four residential areas: central city women averaged $10,886, suburban women $11,908, small town women $9,124, and rural women $9,673. In addition, the average earnings within each occupational group (pay scales) showed differences across the four areas. Now we are ready to ask, are the differentials in average earnings among the residence areas due to differences in pay scales or in occupational distributions? In order to determine which is more important in explaining the differences in average earnings, we employed the Kitagawa (1955) technique of decomposition of rates. We coded occupations into nine categories and computed mean full-time earnings for each category (pay scales) within each residence area. Using occupational structure as "composition" and pay scales as "rates," we compared each residential area to the total group. Table 3.6 presents the two components: the amount of the difference in earnings that is due to effects of occupational distribution and the amount that is due to differences in pay scales. An interaction term between the two components is also included.

Overall, the difference due to pay scales is much larger than the difference due to occupational distribution. The interaction term is negligible in all cases. The importance of the pay scale component varies from one area to the next. In small towns, where average earnings are lowest, the difference in pay scale explains over 86 percent of the difference between earnings of all women and small town women. In other words, if small town women had the same occupational distribution as the total group, their average earnings would be $1,457 less than the total. The rural women have the next lowest average earnings, and almost four-fifths of this difference is due to a lower pay scale. Central city women are very similar in average earnings to the total group because they make up a large proportion of the total. If they had the occupational distribution of the total group, their earnings would be $200 higher than the total. However, if they had the same pay scales as the total, then occupational distribution would lead to $108 less earnings, on average. The suburban women can attribute two-thirds of their higher average earnings to better pay scales, and one-third to a favorable occupational structure.

There are several possible reasons for the low pay scales in small towns and rural areas. The aggregate occupation groupings used here may be masking differences in occupations between urban and rural women; the rural women may be working at the jobs with lower pay scales within each major occupational category. Or the rural women may be working in newer industries with less worker protection and generally lower pay scales. In any case, it seems clear that the small town and rural women are paid less for full-time work than are urban women, and that most of this difference cannot be attributed to differences in occupational structure.

Table 3.6

Components of Earnings Differences for Full-Time Employed Female Family Heads with Minor Children by Urban/Rural Residence, 1979 (total mean earnings = $10,807)

| Components | Urban | | | Small Town | Rural |
|---|---|---|---|---|---|
| | Central City | Suburb | | | |
| Mean wage/salary | $10,886 | $11,908 | | $9,124 | $9,673 |
| Total difference in earnings (area minus total sample) | $79 | $1,101 | | $-1,684 | $-1,134 |
| Difference due to occupational distribution (composition) | -108 | 353 | | -238 | -270 |
| Difference due to pay scales (rates) | 200 | 728 | | -1,457 | -894 |
| Interaction of composition and rates | -13 | 20 | | 11 | 30 |
| Number of cases | 808 | 677 | | 267 | 319 |

## MULTIVARIATE ANALYSIS

In order to examine the multivariate relationships between the independent variables and poverty status as dependent variable, a regression analysis was performed with Multiple Classification Analysis (MCA). This is an Anova type of regression, useful when the dependent variable is dichotomous. The results of this analysis are presented as proportion poor within each category of independent variable (unadjusted mean), and as proportion poor within each category controlling for all other independent variables (adjusted mean) in the equation.

The analysis of the total sample of female family heads is presented in the first two columns of Table 3.7. Age of mother was dropped from the model due to multicollinearity with age of child. Work status in 1979 clearly is the most important variable in terms of explaining variance in poverty status (eta = 0.57). Only 11 percent of women working full-time are in poverty compared with 78 percent of women who did not work in 1979. Education, marital status, and age of children follow in importance. The unadjusted means present no surprises: higher proportions poor occur among unemployed women, women with young children, women who are married with spouse absent, are separated, or single, and women who are nonwhite and less well educated. In general, when the effects of other variables in the model are controlled, the proportion poor (adjusted mean) approaches the grand mean of 42 percent. However, some groups of women remain with over 50 percent living in poverty, i.e., women who are married but husband is absent, women with less than a high school diploma, and women who did not work in 1979. This multivariate model explains 40 percent of the variance in poverty status.

To examine the rural-urban differences, four models were computed, one for each residential area (see Table 3.7). Once again, and after controlling for all other factors in the model, the group of women who had the highest proportion in poverty were those who did not work in 1979. The proportion in poverty among nonworkers ranges from 78 percent in central cities to 66 percent in suburbs. Another work status result is striking: 58 percent of women living in small towns who work part-time live in poverty. We noted in the decompositional analysis that the full-time pay scale for small town workers was much lower than the pay scale in other areas, and we infer that this is also true for part-time workers.

Some other interesting results appear when comparing the different residence groups. Blacks are more likely to be in poverty than whites in all areas; they are also more likely to be poor than are women of other races in suburbs, small towns, and rural areas. However, in central cities, persons of other races have the highest poverty rate.[4]

Finally, having more education reduces the single mother's likelihood of living in poverty, although even after controlling for all of the other vari-

**Table 3.7**
**Multiple Classification Analysis of Poverty Status of Female Family Heads with Minor Children by Urban/Rural Residence, 1980**
(grand mean = 42 percent)

| Characteristic | Unadjusted Mean | Adjusted Mean | | | | |
|---|---|---|---|---|---|---|
| | | Urban | | | | |
| | | Central City | Suburb | Small Town | Rural | Total |
| **Own Children** | | | | | | |
| Some <6 years | 60% | 53% | 42% | 53% | 49% | 49% |
| 6-17 years only | 33 | 45 | 29 | 41 | 38 | 38 |
| Eta | 0.26 | | | | | |
| **Marital Status** | | | | | | |
| Married | 59 | 57 | 44 | 49 | 58 | 52 |
| Divorced | 29 | 45 | 32 | 42 | 43 | 40 |
| Separated | 57 | 52 | 41 | 55 | 54 | 49 |
| Widowed | 32 | 30 | 15 | 32 | 20 | 24 |
| Single | 63 | 54 | 40 | 57 | 47 | 49 |
| Eta | 0.30 | | | | | |
| **Race** | | | | | | |
| White | 34 | 45 | 31 | 44 | 38 | 40 |
| Black | 53 | 49 | 40 | 49 | 52 | 46 |
| Other | 60 | 53 | 34 | 47 | 49 | 46 |
| Eta | 0.20 | | | | | |

Table 3.7 (continued)

| Characteristic | Unadjusted Mean | Adjusted Mean | | | | |
| --- | --- | --- | --- | --- | --- | --- |
| | | Urban | | | | |
| | | Central City | Suburb | Small Town | Rural | Total |
| **Education** | | | | | | |
| 0-11 years | 62 | 55 | 42 | 57 | 46 | 51 |
| 12 years | 36 | 46 | 32 | 43 | 40 | 40 |
| 13+ years | 23 | 39 | 27 | 26 | 33 | 32 |
| Eta | 0.31 | | | | | |
| **Work in 1979** | | | | | | |
| None | 78 | 78 | 66 | 71 | 72 | 72 |
| 1-1749 hours | 49 | 49 | 44 | 58 | 47 | 49 |
| 1750+ hours | 11 | 18 | 9 | 19 | 14 | 15 |
| Eta | 0.57 | | | | | |
| Multiple R Squared | | .414 | .389 | .420 | .360 | .401 |
| Multiple R | | .643 | .624 | .648 | .600 | .633 |
| Number | 5,796 | 2,523 | 1,672 | 721 | 879 | 5,796 |

ables in the model, 39 percent of women with some college education living in central cities are in poverty.

## DISCUSSION

Throughout this analysis it has become apparent that the lives of mothers who head families differ depending on the type of area in which they reside—central city, suburb, small town, or rural area. The women who live in these four areas differ in terms of ages of their children, marital status, race, education, and labor force status. In general, if poverty status is used as the indicator of well-being, suburban mothers are better off than the others and central city mothers are in the worst situation, closely followed by small town and rural women. Since earned income and welfare benefits are the primary sources of income for this population, differences in access to these sources may explain much of the urban-rural variation in poverty status. This chapter focuses on the earned income part of this relationship, noting first that the proportions employed and employed full-time also vary by area of residence. A decomposition of earnings among full-time workers demonstrates that much of the difference in average earnings is due to pay scale differences between urban and rural areas; differences in occupational composition contribute less.

There is a contrast in poverty rates between single mothers who work full- or part-time. However, although working and poverty have a strong inverse relationship, work is not an absolute guarantee of absence of poverty. There are proportionally more full-time workers in towns and rural areas than in the cities. Yet, employed single mothers in small towns and rural areas are more likely to be poor than mothers in cities and suburbs. We suspect that the motivations and access to work differ across the four residential areas. In addition, not all single mothers can attain an above-poverty wage, even when working full-time.

Research has shown that persons in cities, including single mothers, have better access to welfare benefits. Thus, women living in central cities may have a more evident option to employment as a means of supporting a family. Coupled with the lower age and presumed lower levels of work force experience, there also may be less advantage in employment for these mothers.

Suburban single mothers are the most likely to be working. Their higher educational attainment along with higher pay scales make employment a generally attractive means of supporting a family.

Small town women may find fewer alternatives to employment, even though the pay scales for full-time workers are the lowest of all four residence areas. Also, there may be more stigma associated with welfare or more acceptance of work as the way to support a family.

The largest proportion of older mothers as well as widows live in rural areas. Social Security and Supplemental Security Income benefits as well as employment contribute to their income. There may be important differences in their access to jobs, as compared to other single mothers.

Public policy has varied during the last twenty years, sometimes encouraging single mothers to stay at home with their children, sometimes encouraging work outside the home. Along with these mixed messages, individual circumstances complicate any clarity that is present in the policy. Single mothers bear the responsibility of supporting a family; some mothers have choices in carrying out this responsibility and others have little freedom of choice. While support from absent fathers, welfare benefits, and social security are important income sources for many, employment is becoming the most important option that is within their control. The latest research has indicated that the proportion of women who work continues to increase, even among those with preschool children (Waite 1981; O'Connell and Bloom 1987).

This research suggests that the most important factor for not living in poverty is earning income. Most single mothers (70 percent) work. Those who work full-time are the least likely to live in poverty, followed by those who work part-time. However, even among women who work full-time, 11 percent are living in poverty. Among part-time workers, the poverty rate rises to 49 percent. With a detailed analysis of average income by occupation and residence among full-time workers, we discovered that differentials in income among the four residential groups were less likely to be due to the types of jobs available (the occupational structure) than to the differences in pay scales for the same occupational level. Thus, one way to reduce poverty among single mothers who work is to raise the minimum wage on a national basis. Efforts currently under way to raise the minimum wage will probably do more to decrease poverty than would increases in welfare benefits. Other policy efforts to increase women's equity in the labor market would also have widespread implications for the reduction of poverty among mothers and children. The most important of these efforts include broad child care provisions, both through employers and through governmental support; access to education and training programs; increased enforcement of child support responsibilities for absent parents; and increasing pay equity between men and women. None of these initiatives can occur easily, but any one of them—implemented on a national scale—would have a major impact on the decline of poverty in the future.

## NOTES

1. Urban and rural are concepts based primarily on population size of places (cities, towns, villages).

I. URBAN
  A. Urbanized area: a concentration of at least 50,000 people, which usually includes a central city and surrounding, closely settled suburbs. Generally, population density is 1,000 or more persons per square mile.
      1. Central city: the largest incorporated place within the UA, plus all other cities that have at least one-third the population of the largest city, or which have 250,000 or more inhabitants.
      2. Urban fringe: the remainder of the UA, outside the central city.
  B. Outside urbanized area: all places of 2,500 or more persons that are not inside the urbanized areas. Generally, this includes places of 2,500 to 50,000 inhabitants.
II. RURAL
  This includes all persons not living in an urban area. This includes places of less than 2,500 inhabitants and sparsely settled areas.

Further details can be found in the U.S. Bureau of the Census (1982).

2. The Public Use Microdata C Sample (PUMS) from the 1980 U.S. Census of Population and Housing is used for this analysis. The C Sample was specifically selected because it allows an urban/rural classification that is not possible with the other PUMS samples. The original PUMS C sample for 1980 contains over 800,000 household records, with associated person records. The subsample used in this analysis was drawn in a series of steps. (1) All group quarters records were excluded. (2) Remaining households were divided into two groups: urban and rural. Ten percent of urban and 20 percent of rural households with a female householder were randomly selected. The resulting sample sizes were 18,725 urban, and 7,594 rural, for a total of 26,319 households headed by a female. These samples were then weighted to return them to the proportions that they represent in the population. The weight applied to urban cases was 1.1686; rural cases were weighted by 0.5843. The result was 21,882 urban households and 4,437 rural households (a total again of 26,319 households). (3) All family households headed by a woman with no husband present that included minor children of the head were selected, resulting in a weighted total of 5,796 households.

These cases are a stratified random sample of all family households headed by women with children and with no husband present. Further details are found in Slesinger and Cautley (1986).

3. This is equivalent to working thirty-five or more hours for fifty or more weeks. This is a product of two variables: weeks worked during 1979 multiplied by the usual hours worked per week. It is thus an estimate of the actual hours worked during 1979.

4. It should be noted that there are fewer than 200 nonwhite women in both the small towns and the rural areas in this sample.

**REFERENCES**

Bianchi, Suzanne M., and Daphne Spain. 1986. *American Women in Transition.* A Census Monograph Series. New York: Russell Sage Foundation.

Deavers, Kenneth L., Robert A. Hoppe, and Peggy J. Ross. 1986. "Public Policy and Rural Poverty: A View from the 1980s." *Policy Studies Journal* 15(2):291-309.

Garfinkel, Irwin, and Sara S. McLanahan. 1985. "The Feminization of Poverty: Nature, Causes, and a Partial Cure." Discussion paper 776-85, Institute for Research on Poverty. Madison, Wis.: University of Wisconsin.

_____. 1986. *Single Mothers and Their Children: A New American Dilemma.* Washington, D.C.: Urban Institute Press.

Kitagawa, Evelyn M. 1955. "Components of a Difference between Two Rates." *Journal of the American Statistical Association* 50:1168-94.

O'Connell, Martin, and David E. Bloom. 1987. "Cutting the Apron Strings: Women in the Labor Force in the 1980s." Discussion paper 87-1, Center for Population Studies. Cambridge, Mass.: Harvard University.

Oppenheimer, Valerie K. 1970. *The Female Labor Force in the United States.* Population Monograph Series, no. 5, Berkeley: University of California.

Ross, Peggy J., and Elizabeth S. Morrissey. 1986. "Persistent Poverty among the Nonmetropolitan Poor." Paper given at Southern Rural Sociological Association, February 4, Orlando, Fla.

Slesinger, Doris P., and Eleanor Cautley. 1986. "Determinants of Poverty among Rural and Urban Women Who Live Alone." Working paper 86-43, Center for Demography and Ecology. Madison, Wis.: University of Wisconsin-Madison.

Taeuber, Cynthia M., and Victor Valdisera. 1986. "Women in the American Economy." *Current Population Reports,* Special Studies Series P-23, no. 146. U.S. Bureau of the Census. Washington, D.C.: U.S. Government Printing Office.

U.S. Bureau of the Census. 1982. *User's Guide: Part B, Glossary.* 1980 Census of Population and Housing, PHC80-R1-B. Washington, D.C.: U.S. Government Printing Office.

U.S. Bureau of the Census. 1983. *1980 Census of Population and Housing, General Social and Economic Characteristics, United States Summary.* Vol. 1, ch. C, PC80-1-C1, Washington, D.C.: U.S. Government Printing Office.

Waite, Linda J. 1981. "U.S. Women at Work." *Population Bulletin* 36(2). Washington, D.C.: Population Reference Bureau.

# 4

# Impacts of the Farm Financial Crisis of the 1980s on Resources and Poverty in Agriculturally Dependent Counties in the United States

STEVE H. MURDOCK, F. LARRY LEISTRITZ,
RITA R. HAMM, DON E. ALBRECHT,
LLOYD POTTER, and KENNETH BACKMAN

During the early part of the 1980s, agriculture in the United States experienced its most severe financial crisis since the Great Depression. As a result of low commodity prices, falling values for assets (particularly land), high interest rates, a strong U.S. dollar, an increase in world commodity supplies, and similar factors, many producers were forced from agriculture and many others faced substantial financial problems (Murdock and Leistritz 1988; Johnson et al. 1986; Reimund and Petrulis 1987). As a result, the term "farm crisis" came into prominence as a means of referring to the condition of high proportions of agricultural producers being under unusually high levels of financial stress (usually defined as a debt-to-asset ratio of 40 percent or higher) and local, state, and national policymakers expressed increasing levels of concern about the effects of the crisis on agricultural producers and rural areas. Researchers also began to focus their efforts on assessing the impacts of the crisis on producers and rural communities (Murdock and Leistritz 1988; Korsching and Gildner 1986).

Although the base of knowledge regarding the characteristics of the farming operations and of the producers who have been impacted is increasing (Murdock et al. 1985; Leholm et al. 1985; Albrecht et al. 1987a, 1987b; Heffernan and Heffernan 1985; Bultena et al. 1986) and an increasing, yet extremely limited, base of information is accumulating on the effects of the crisis on rural communities and their residents (Murdock and Leistritz 1988; Murdock et al. 1987; Albrecht et al. 1988; Doeksen 1987; Heffernan and Heffernan 1985), the effects of the crisis on the general social and economic welfare of rural areas has not been adequately examined. As a result, the effects that the crisis has had, or may yet have, on the ability of residents in rural areas to maintain an adequate base of resources to support individual households and to support community services in rural areas remain unclear.

Analysis of the effects of the farm financial crisis on the general welfare of rural areas is critical for several reasons. First, many of the areas being impacted by the crisis have social and economic characteristics that make them extremely vulnerable to declines in their income and other aspects of their economic and social service bases. Thus, rural economies have not only experienced declines in their agricultural bases, but because of the disproportionate involvement of their economies in low-wage manufacturing and in such natural resource industries as forestry and mining, which have also experienced rapid downturns in the 1980s, their alternative bases for support outside of production agriculture have been severely weakened (Bloomquist 1987; Henry et al. 1986).

In like manner, the often heralded renewed population growth in rural areas, prevalent in the 1970s, appears to have reverted in the 1980s to the historical pattern of net outmigration from rural to urban areas (Richter 1985; Engels 1986; Brown and Deavers 1987). As a result of such patterns, continued population loss in rural areas appears to be taking its traditional toll on rural services such as rural hospitals, schools, and commercial businesses (Long et al. 1987; Johnson 1985). For many of those areas most dependent on agriculture, in fact, the turnaround was either not experienced at all or was experienced at sharply reduced rates of growth compared to other nonmetropolitan areas (Bender et al. 1985; Fuguitt 1985).

As a result of these trends and other historical and economic conditions, in 1985 the poverty rate in nonmetropolitan areas in the United States was 18.3 percent compared to 12.7 percent in metropolitan areas; for both types of areas, the rate has increased substantially since the late 1970s (Brown and Deavers 1987; Deavers et al. 1986). Although a majority of poverty counties are still in nonmetropolitan areas in the South, poverty is becoming increasingly prevalent in nonmetropolitan areas in other regions of the nation during the 1980s. Compounding the problems of low income has been the fact that those populations experiencing the most severe resource problems have disproportionate numbers of female-headed households and minority households, which have the most limited access to the resources and opportunities necessary to improve their resource bases (Morrissey 1985).

In addition, as shown in Table 4.1, counties that are most directly dependent on agriculture have lower levels of health and similar basic services, higher percentages of youth and elderly living in poverty, older housing

**Table 4.1**
**Selected Characteristics of Agriculturally Dependent Counties\* and Other Nonmetropolitan and Metropolitan Counties, 1980**

| Selected Characteristics | County Type | | | |
| --- | --- | --- | --- | --- |
| | Agriculturally Dependent Counties | Other Nonmetro Counties | Metropolitan Counties | All U.S. Counties |
| Total population | 4,081,088 | 53,034,094 | 169,430,623 | 226,545,805 |
| Percent | | | | |
| Urban | 21.7 | 38.1 | 85.3 | 73.7 |
| Rural | 78.3 | 61.9 | 14.7 | 26.3 |
| Rural farm | 19.2 | 6.6 | 1.0 | 2.5 |
| < 18 years of age | 30.2 | 29.4 | 27.7 | 28.1 |
| 18–24 years of age | 10.9 | 12.7 | 13.5 | 13.3 |
| 25–34 years of age | 13.6 | 14.9 | 16.9 | 16.4 |
| 35–44 years of age | 10.2 | 10.7 | 11.5 | 11.3 |
| 45–54 years of age | 9.9 | 10.7 | 10.2 | 10.1 |
| 55–64 years of age | 10.4 | 7.3 | 9.5 | 9.6 |
| 65+ years of age | 14.9 | 12.9 | 10.7 | 11.2 |
| Black | 6.7 | 9.0 | 12.6 | 11.7 |
| Spanish-origin | 6.9 | 2.8 | 7.5 | 6.5 |
| Number of households | 1,431,238 | 17,357,039 | 61,601,325 | 80,389,602 |
| Average size of household | 2.9 | 2.9 | 2.8 | 2.8 |
| Physicians per 100,000 population, 1980 | 53.12 | 93.94 | 225.99 | 193.84 |
| Hospital beds per 100,000 population, 1980 | 434.79 | 576.00 | 625.01 | 610.81 |

Table 4.1 (continued)

| Selected Characteristics | County Type | | | |
| --- | --- | --- | --- | --- |
| | Agriculturally Dependent Counties | Other Nonmetro Counties | Metropolitan Counties | All U.S. Counties |
| Police officers per 1,000 population, 1980 | 1.37 | 1.38 | 2.03 | 1.87 |
| Percent of housing units vacant, 1980 | 10.75 | 10.01 | 6.38 | 7.27 |
| Percent of housing units without complete plumbing, 1980 | 4.26 | 4.30 | 1.52 | 2.17 |
| Percent owner occupied, 1980 | 74.40 | 73.16 | 61.74 | 64.43 |
| Percent renter occupied, 1980 | 22.85 | 24.15 | 35.82 | 32.98 |
| Percent of 1980 housing units built from 1970-80 | 23.8 | 28.7 | 25.6 | 26.2 |
| Percent of 1980 housing units built 1939 or earlier | 38.9 | 30.4 | 24.2 | 25.9 |
| Median years of school completed for persons 25+, 1980 | 12.30 | 12.20 | 12.40 | 12.30 |
| Total revenue (total taxes) per capita, 1982 | $366.90 | $304.80 | $490.65 | $447.72 |
| Debt outstanding per capita, 1982 | $673.45 | $871.39 | $1,187.63 | $1,109.18 |
| Per capita money income, 1979 | $5,610 | $5,938 | $7,727 | $7,295 |

**Table 4.1** (continued)

| Selected Characteristics | County Type | | | |
| --- | --- | --- | --- | --- |
| | Agriculturally Dependent Counties | Other Nonmetro Counties | Metropolitan Counties | All U.S. Counties |
| Percent of population receiving Social Security benefits, 1980 | 19.24 | 17.90 | 14.47 | 15.31 |
| Percent of persons below poverty, 1979 | 17.75 | 15.06 | 11.10 | 12.09 |
| Percent of persons 65+ below poverty, 1979 | 20.24 | 19.89 | 11.77 | 14.02 |
| Percent of persons <18 below poverty, 1979 | 21.77 | 18.36 | 14.77 | 15.73 |
| Bank savings per capita, 1980 | $816 | $831 | $1,207 | $1,117 |
| Savings and loan savings per capita, 1979 | $842 | $1,223 | $2,243 | $1,993 |
| Retail sales per capita, 1982 | $2,977 | $3,888 | $4,982 | $4,705 |
| Manufacturing payroll per capita, 1979 | $344 | $1,049 | $1,616 | $1,468 |

*The categorization of counties shown in this table was devised using the procedures described in the methodology section of this chapter.

stocks, fewer financial resources, and less developed retail service structures
to serve their populations than urban areas or other nonagriculturally based
nonmetropolitan areas (Murdock et al. 1988). In like manner, an analysis of
the data in Table 4.1 suggests that populations in agriculturally dependent
counties have heavier dependency burdens, with 30 percent of their populations under the age of eighteen and nearly 15 percent sixty-five years of age
or older compared to 27 percent under eighteen years of age and 10 percent
sixty-five years of age or older in metropolitan counties in 1980. A growing
body of literature also suggests that services in rural areas have deteriorated
in the 1980s (Doeksen and Peterson 1987) and that rural areas have received
decreasing amounts of federal resources in the 1980s and have disproportionately experienced the effects of federal budget cuts (Long et al. 1987).

The need to examine such secondary impacts as those on the general
welfare of rural areas is also suggested by the fact that the recent increase in
agricultural incomes and commodity prices (Johnson et al. 1987) appear to
be leading to a growing public sentiment that the farm crisis is over. This is
evident in the reduced coverage of the crisis in the popular press and in the
professional journals of agriculturally oriented disciplines (*Successful
Farming* 1988). Because growing public recognition of the crisis resulted in
a relatively large number of state assistance programs (Popovich 1987) and
financial institutions and the federal government have been increasingly
willing to renegotiate and/or cancel the existing loan obligations for some
agricultural producers, many believe that the problems resulting from the
farm crisis have been addressed to the extent possible within the guise of
public policy. Although the recent drought has clearly increased the vulner-
ability of many highly leveraged producers, for many in the general public
drought assistance is presumed, inaccurately, to have alleviated the impacts
of the drought. In fact, there is little doubt that the drought will increase the
rate and pace of farm failure in the United States.

Such perspectives fail to recognize the fact that the crisis is a rural
crisis—not only a farm crisis—and that the rural communities dependent on
agriculture are likely to be most affected by the indirect and induced impacts
that develop slowly and only after the direct impacts on agricultural
producers have become apparent (or perhaps have even begun to dissipate).
For these sectors of the rural economy and for many of the social and cultural
organizations in rural areas, it appears that many of the most severe impacts
have become evident only in the mid-1980s and may continue for several
years into the future (Albrecht 1988; Albrecht et al. 1988). For the service and
fiscal bases of such communities, for example, the problems of public
provision and financing of services have only recently become apparent
(Stinson et al. 1986). The potential effects on rural organizations and communities of the loss of substantial proportions of their human resource base is
likely to be evident in reduced membership and fiscal stability for these
organizations and, for both organizations and the communities at large, a

loss of substantial numbers of community and organizational leaders (Murdock et al. 1988). The operators and employees of rural businesses, and general public and private-sector service structures of many rural communities, are also continuing to experience the effects of the crisis as sales decline and the support for local employment is lost.

The loss of income and support for the service base resulting from the indirect and induced effects of the farm financial crisis may destroy the viability of many rural areas to provide quality living environments and to retain the base necessary for redevelopment, and the impacts on such areas are likely to be ignored due to a growing belief that the crisis is abating. Thus, identification of the nature and magnitude of the impacts of the farm crisis on the general welfare of rural areas is absolutely essential. Unless the impacts are identified and their likely magnitude established, policymakers may not become aware of such impacts and may not develop appropriate programs to address these impacts.

This chapter identifies the types and the potential magnitude of the impacts likely to result from the farm crisis in agriculturally dependent areas in the United States. Specificially, the types of impacts the crisis may have on the population and on the economic and service bases of agriculturally dependent counties are examined and then the potential effects of the crisis on the income bases of such areas are evaluated. The analysis is limited to agriculturally dependent counties because it is in these areas that the impacts are most likely to be experienced. Any analysis of the impacts of the crisis for the rural sector as a whole or for nonmetropolitan America as a whole will likely find such impacts to be relatively small but will also fail to recognize the disproportionate distributional effects of the crisis. The intent here is to identify such impact in those agriculturally dependent areas where the effects of the farm financial crisis are most likely to have significant implications and to add to the base of information essential to the formation of effective policy to address the needs of such areas.

## METHODOLOGY

The analysis reported in this chapter involved the use of two general bodies of data and several admittedly speculative assumptions about the potential impacts of the crisis on agriculturally dependent areas and rural residents in the coming years. It also involved the development of procedures for determining agriculturally dependent areas and for tracing the impacts in these areas.

Data on the financial characteristics of U.S. producers as a whole and on the number of such producers were obtained from the work of Johnson and others in the U.S. Department of Agriculture (1985 and 1986). To obtain detailed information on the characteristics of agricultural producers and other rural residents, generalizations were made from data sets collected by the authors in several survey efforts conducted in 1985, 1986, and 1987 in Texas and North Dakota.

In March through May of 1985, random sample telephone surveys of producers in North Dakota and Texas were conducted. The sampling frames for these surveys were taken from those used by governmental agencies involved in periodic surveys of producers in the two states. Common survey instruments were used in the two states. A total of 1,953 operators were interviewed (933 in North Dakota and 1,020 in Texas); the overall response rate was 75 percent (70 percent in Texas and 77 percent in North Dakota). Respondents were screened to obtain a sample of persons having farming or ranching as their major economic enterprise and for whom the financial situation in agriculture was likely to have long-term consequences. Interviews were limited to persons under sixty-five years of age who operated a farm or ranch at the time of the interview, who had gross farm sales of more than $2,500 in 1984, and who considered farming to be their primary occupation. Standard telephone survey techniques involving three callbacks at different times of the day and different days of the week were used. The sample sizes were sufficient to allow response patterns to be estimated within 10 percent of the likely population response with a 95-percent level of confidence. Comparisons of the characteristics of the survey respondents to those for the farm population in 1980 and the characteristics of farm operators from the 1982 Census of Agriculture indicated that the respondents were generally representative of producers operating commercial-sized farms in the two states (Murdock et al. 1985; Leholm et al. 1985).

The questionnaire elicited informatin on a wide variety of financial, demographic, and perceptual information on the operators and financial and structural information on the farm firm. The instruments also obtained information on relatives or others who would always know the producer's residence even if he or she no longer lived at the residence occupied at the time of the survey. This latter item was collected to allow for subsequent follow-up studies.

In the spring and summer of 1986, follow-up surveys of producers in each of the states were completed. These surveys were of the same basic form as those used in 1985, but in addition to the information collected in 1985, these instruments solicited information on producers' evaluations of the impacts of the crisis on their communities, on themselves, and on their families. As with the original survey, a telephone interview was again used with a minimum of three callbacks.

In Texas, 961 (94 percent) of the 1,020 producers who were interviewed in 1985 were recontacted in 1986. Of the 961 contacted, a total of 815 interviews were completed (85 percent of the 961 and 79.9 percent of the original sample). The completed interviews included 791 farmers who were still farming and 24 persons who had left farming during the year. An additional

137 respondents refused to be interviewed, and 9 producers had either died between 1985 and 1986 or were medically unable to participate in the 1986 survey. Of the 137, it was possible to establish that 116 were still farming and 21 had left agriculture. In North Dakota, 759 (81.4 percent) of the 933 operators interviewed in 1985 were reinterviewed in 1986 with the remaining 174 consisting of persons who refused (99 respondents), could not be contacted (53 respondents), had ceased to operate farms (18 respondents), or were deceased (4 respondents).

A former farmer survey was also conducted during the latter part of 1986 in North Dakota only. A list of 432 producers who had quit farming was selected from lists obtained from agencies that have frequent contacts with producers. Because neither a uniform nor comprehensive list of former producers could be obtained, this was not a random sample and may be biased in unknown ways. Given the sparsity of data on former producers, however, this represented a unique data set, which we believe is useful for discerning the likely characteristics and responses of former producers.

Of the 432 producers for whom names were obtained, 260 were contacted by phone and the remainder were mailed questionnaires. Altogether, 169 usable questionnaires (39.1 percent of the total 432) were obtained. Although this response rate is much lower than in the other surveys and is much lower than desired, these former producers showed little desire to be interviewed. For many, the experience of leaving farming was extremely painful, and they did not wish to complete a survey about the events related to it, despite repeated attempts to obtain a response. The questionnaire for this survey asked questions related to the characteristics of their farm during its last years of operation, about steps they had taken to restructure their farming operations, and about the general impacts of the crisis on them and their communities.

The final two surveys used in the chapter involve surveys of business operators and former business operators and of community residents in nine communities (six in North Dakota and three in Texas) conducted in the summer and fall of 1986 in North Dakota and in the fall of 1986 and the spring of 1987 in Texas. These communities ranged in population size from 1,700 to 16,000. In all communities an attempt was made to interview all current business operators, to locate and interview former business operators, and to interview approximately one hundred residents in each community. For community residents, this number of respondents was of a sufficient size to provide 95-percent confidence that the estimate was within 10 percent of the population response in each community. Resident interviews were restricted to persons who were not business operators and who did not own or operate a farm. All three surveys were restricted to persons who were less than sixty-five years of age and not retired and could thus be assumed to depend on the community for a majority of their livelihood.

In the completion of the business operator survey, 1,417 businesses were contacted in the nine communities. Of these operators, 715 or 50.5 percent responded with response rates varying from 39.6 percent to 63.4 percent among the communities. This relatively low response rate was the result of the detailed financial information requested in the survey instrument. Many operators simply refused to provide such detailed information.

Altogether, 143 former business operators were identified, and 77 (53.9 percent) responded. As with former producers, many former business operators did not wish to respond to a survey that required them to relive a painful experience. In the nine communities, 1,153 residents were contacted; 829 or 71.9 percent responded to the survey. Response rates varied from 59.8 percent to 87.0 percent among the communities.

The current and former business operators' questionnaires requested participants to provide information on financial and other characteristics of their business and on their perceptions of the farm crisis and its impacts on them and their communities. The survey of residents examined items similar to those in the business surveys with the exception of the detailed business-related questions. All surveys obtained detailed information on the demographic and economic characteristics of the respondent and the respondent's household.

Although the data reported above are clearly limited to two states and to various extents by the nature of the samples on which they are based, they were the most complete information known to the authors at the time the analysis reported here was completed. They were thus used in the analysis of the impacts of the crisis reported here. It was assumed that the combined 1986 producer and former producer survey results applied to all producers, and survey data on business operators, former business operators, and residents were combined and assumed to apply to other persons in agriculturally dependent counties.

The overall impacts of the crisis on resources were determined by the use of assumptions about the number of producers who would be forced to leave farming between now and the year 1995 and about the direct and indirect effects of the loss of agricultural producers on secondary commercial, service, and income structures in rural areas. In fact, it was necessary to make a number of very speculative assumptions. We made assumptions about the proportion of producers who will leave farming and rural areas in the coming years, about the proportion of sales that will be lost to rural communities due to the loss of these producers, about the numbers of persons (both producers and related secondary worker populations) who will migrate from rural areas due to the crisis, and about the implications of the loss of alternative numbers of persons from rural areas. For each of these factors, we made assumptions that extend beyond the base of existing knowledge. Thus, there is a limited empirical base of evidence from which to estimate the exact proportion of producers with different levels of debt who will actually fail in the coming years, about the time period over which those producers who fail will leave farming, or about the local area impacts of such a loss.

It is clear, for example, that some producers with even the highest levels of debt may be able to restructure that debt and remain in farming. In addition, in nearly all cases, the land farmed by producers who fail will remain in production (albeit under the direction of new operators). As a result, many of the expenditures associated with production activities (e.g., purchases of fertilizers and seed) will continue to be made even if they are made by a smaller number of producers. The economic impacts of the loss of a given number of producers cannot therefore be easily estimated by the use of a simple export-base multiplier.

We are therefore under no illusion that the implications estimated will reflect the actual course of events that will result from the crisis. Rather, we believe that an examination of a range of potential implications of the crisis, even if based on rather speculative assumptions, is essential for discerning the types and magnitude of policy actions that should be formulated to address such implications. The specific assumptions and limitations imposed on the analysis are as follows.

First, the analysis is restricted to the potential implications of farm failure for agriculturally dependent counties. Following the lead of Bender et al. (1985), we define agriculturally dependent counties as those nonmetropolitan counties in which 20 percent or more of total earnings comes from agriculture. However, whereas Bender et al. utilized a weighted average of income and employment from 1975 to 1979 and the designation of metropolitan areas as delineated in 1974, we utilize average earnings from agriculture in 1976, 1980, and 1983 and the metropolitan designation used for the 1980 Census. We made these alterations of the procedures utilized by Bender et al. because we deemed it desirable—because the farm crisis had its origins in the events of the late 1970s but is having its most obvious impacts in the mid-1980s—to utilize data that would span the period of time from the late 1970s to the beginning of the 1980s. The procedures utilized provide a set of counties with agricultural involvement throughout the major period of the evolution of the causes and consequences of the crisis.

The period chosen for measuring agricultural dependence is important because of the rapid decline that has occurred in the number of agriculturally dependent counties. If the 1980 delineation of metropolitan status and the 20-percent criteria are used, 639 counties can be identified as agriculturally dependent in 1976; by 1983, this number is only 362. There has thus been a rapid decline in agriculture as an income source in the United States during the early 1980s. We utilized the metropolitan designation in 1980 because a majority of the other data used in the analysis presented below are from the 1980 Census. These procedures resulted in 472 nonmetropolitan counties being identified as agriculturally dependent. Throughout the analysis, events in these agriculturally dependent counties are contrasted to those in other nonmetropolitan counties, in metropolitan counties, and in all U.S. counties.

Perhaps the most critical assumption in terms of the analysis is that related to the number of producers who will be forced to leave agriculture. Although any such estimate must clearly be speculative, existing analyses (Dunn 1987; Ginder 1985; Goreham et al. 1987; Marousek 1979; Barry 1986) suggest that a majority of those who have debt-to-asset ratios of more than 70 percent will be unable to remain in farming and that a significant percentage of those in the 41-to-70 percent debt-to-asset ratio category may also be forced to leave agriculture. Using the estimates for 1985 of the number of farms by debt-to-asset ratio of Johnson et al. (1986), we assume that all of those who have debt-to-asset ratios exceeding 100 percent will be forced from farming (such producers are in fact already insolvent), that 75 percent of those with debt-to-asset ratios of from 70 to 100 percent will fail, and that 50 percent of those with debt-to-asset ratios of from 41 to 70 percent will fail. Although admittedly simplistic, given that the estimates by Johnson et al. (1986) do not address failure among smaller U.S. farms because these are largely omitted from his survey efforts, we believe that these estimates of the number of farms likely to fail are probably conservative.

An estimation of the secondary effects of the loss of a given number of producers is equally difficult to complete because it is evident that many of the secondary impacts of expenditures in agriculture occur outside rural farming areas. As a result, relatively conservative assumptions have been made about the secondary effects of the failure of producers. Given that total multipliers for agriculture tend to vary from 2.5 to nearly 4.0 when the location of such impacts is not considered and given that most analysis of the secondary impacts of resource-based developments in rural areas (see Murdock et al. 1986) show that the multiplier effects in local rural areas are often less than 2.0 (including the direct worker), we have made two alternative assumptions concerning secondary employment loss resulting from the loss of producers in agriculturally dependent rural areas. These assumptions attempt to simultaneously take into account that our interest is in secondary impacts only within agriculturally dependent counties themselves and in those secondary effects resulting from the workers who will be forced to leave these counties as a result of the crisis. The alternative assumptions used are that for each producer lost, either 0.25 secondary workers (Scenario I) or 0.75 secondary workers (Scenario II) will be lost from agriculturally dependent counties. The use of these assumptions results in the estimation that between 53,000 and 160,000 secondary workers could be lost from agriculturally dependent rural areas as a result of farm failure in these areas.

Given the assumptions about the number of producers and secondary workers who will leave agriculturally dependent nonmetropolitan counties as a result of the crisis, the remainder of the analysis was completed by examining the implications of the loss of producers and secondary workers on the resources of such areas. This was done by using data on the agricultural, economic, demographic, public service, fiscal, and social characteristics of such counties derived from the 1980 Census of Population and Housing and the 1982 Censuses of Agriculture, Government, and Business; by utilizing data from the North Dakota and Texas surveys of producers, former producers, current and former business operators, and community residents; and by using data from the U.S. Department of Agriculture on the characteristics of producers with alternative levels of debt in 1985 (Johnson et al. 1986). We assume that those producers who will leave agriculturally dependent counties will have the average characteristics of producers with high debt-to-asset ratios and of producers who have already been forced to leave farming during the mid-1980s. Average characteristics of former producers and of those in our surveys with debt-to-asset ratios exceeding 40 percent are used to measure the likely demographic characteristics of producers who will leave agriculture in the coming years.

Estimating the characteristics of secondary workers posed other problems. Because of the relatively small sample size in our former business surveys (only 83) and the fact that many who will leave will likely not be business operators but other community residents, we used the average characteristics of all respondents in our community surveys (former and current business operators as well as other community residents) as the assumed characteristics of the secondary workers who would leave agriculturally dependent counties in the years to come.

To assess the direct impacts on agriculture, we used data from Johnson et al. (1986) on the characteristics of producers with high debt-to-asset ratios (more than 40 percent) in 1985, and we subtracted the estimated number of producers with specific characteristics from the total number of producers with such characteristics in agriculturally dependent counties as indicated in the 1982 Census of Agriculture. To assess the demographic impacts of the loss, we estimated population loss by applying our assumptions about the demographic characteristics of those who will be forced to leave rural areas (such as their average household size, number of dependents under eighteen years of age, and the age distribution of the producers and their families) and applied these to the number of producers and secondary workers assumed to be leaving agriculturally dependent rural areas. These projected total population effects were then examined in relation to 1980 Census data for such counties. Because of the relatively young age distribution of the producer and secondary worker populations being examined, we do not attempt to survive or otherwise extend the demographic groups for 1980 to 1995 before making comparisons. Rather, impacts were examined relative to the characteristics of populations in agriculturally dependent counties in 1980. Other impacts were projected largely on a per population unit basis given the number of persons projected to leave rural areas.

## FINDINGS

As a first means of examining the results of this analysis, it is useful to examine the validity of the categorization of agriculturally dependent counties. This can be done by examining the data in Tables 4.1 and 4.2. The description of the data in Table 4.1 shows that those counties categorized as agriculturally dependent clearly have distinct social and economic characteristics, and the data in Table 4.2 indicate that these counties have economies based in agriculture. As shown in Table 4.2, these counties had 284,341 farms with an average size of 889 acres, and 63 percent of these farms had sales of $40,000 or more, the sales category usually associated with commercial-scale farming (Johnson et al. 1985). The operators of these farms worked fewer days off the farm, and their per capita earnings from agriculture were more than twice the earnings of persons in the other county categories. The data in Table 4.2 suggest that the counties identified as agriculturally dependent are indeed agricultural.

The projections of the demographic impacts of the alternative levels of farm failure are shown in Table 4.3. As shown in the data in this table, more than 213,500 producers, or 13.8 percent of all producers in the nation, could be forced from agriculture under these projections; if these persons were forced to relocate in areas outside of agriculturally dependent rural areas, more than 800,000 producers and dependents could be dislocated from such areas. Under conservative assumptions of secondary related effects likely to result from the loss of producers, an additional 165,000 to 496,000 persons could be dislocated. In total, between 976,000 and 1,307,000 persons—between 23.9 and 32.0 percent of the total population in agriculturally dependent rural areas—could be lost from these areas due to the crisis. Analyses not reported here (see Murdock et al. 1988) suggest that the producers and secondary workers affected would be largely young adults with families and that consequently, their dislocation would result in a disproportionate loss of young adults and children from agriculturally dependent areas and would remove a significant proportion of the human resource base involved in community organizations and the leadership of such organizations in such areas. For example, these estimates indicate that between 200,000 and 275,000 school children could be lost from schools which, in many cases, are already struggling to maintain enrollments sufficiently large enough to maintain their economic feasibility. In addition, when one considers that the average rural community in 1980 had 800 persons, the population losses projected would be equivalent to the death of more than 600 rural trade centers. Clearly effects of this relative magnitude would markedly affect the resource base in agriculturally dependent rural areas.

Tables 4.4 and 4.5 indicate the potential effects of the crisis on the financial resources of the institutions and residents of agriculturally dependent counties in the United States assuming per capita values from the 1980 and

**Table 4.2**
**Selected Agricultural Characteristics of Agriculturally Dependent Nonmetropolitan Counties, Other Nonmetropolitan Counties, Metropolitan Counties, and All U.S. Counties, 1980 and 1982**

| | County Type | | | |
|---|---|---|---|---|
| Selected Characteristics | Agriculturally Dependent Counties | Other Nonmetro Counties | Metropolitan Counties | All U.S. Counties |
| Number of farms | 284,341 | 1,308,359 | 648,276 | 2,240,976 |
| Percent of farms with sales: | | | | |
| < $10,000 | 28.5 | 49.8 | 56.4 | 49.0 |
| $10,000–$19,999 | 12.1 | 11.9 | 10.7 | 11.6 |
| $20,000–$39,999 | 15.6 | 11.1 | 9.1 | 11.1 |
| $40,000+ | 43.8 | 27.2 | 23.8 | 28.3 |
| $100,000+ | 19.9 | 12.8 | 12.2 | 13.5 |
| Farmland as a percent of total land | 77.4 | 37.4 | 39.2 | 43.5 |
| Average size of farm (acres) | 889 | 437 | 249 | 440 |
| Average value of farm, land and buildings | $483,514 | $312,383 | $352,841 | $345,801 |
| Percent working 100+ days off-farm | 31.8 | 47.1 | 53.3 | 47.0 |
| Per capita earnings ($) from agriculture, forestry and fisheries | 59.7 | 22.5 | 21.1 | 22.0 |

**Table 4.3**
**Projected Demographic Impacts of Alternative Levels of Farm Failure in the United States**

Number of Producers Lost by Debt-to-Asset Ratio Category

| Debt-to-Asset Ratio | Assumed Percentage Leaving Agriculture[1] (1985-1995) | Number of Producers in the U.S. in 1985 | Number Assumed to Leave Agriculture[1] (1985-1995) | Percent of All Producers in the U.S. (1,551,000)[2] |
|---|---|---|---|---|
| > 1.00 | 100 | 61,000 | 61,000 | 3.9 |
| .71-1.00 | 75 | 72,000 | 54,000 | 3.5 |
| .41-.70 | 50 | 197,000 | 98,500 | 6.4 |
| Total | --- | 330,000 | 213,500 | 13.8 |

Producer-Related Population Lost

| Producers Lost | Assumed Household Size[3] | Total Population Lost |
|---|---|---|
| 213,500 | 3.8 | 811,300 |

Table 4.3 (continued)

| Scenarios | Assumptions | Secondary Workers Assumed to Leave Agriculturally Dependent Counties | Assumed Household Size[3] | Secondary Worker Related Population Lost |
|---|---|---|---|---|
| I | .25 secondary workers leave area for every producer leaving the area | 53,375 | 3.1 | 165,463 |
| II | .75 secondary workers leave area for every producer leaving the area | 160,125 | 3.1 | 496,388 |

**Population Change in Agriculturally Dependent Rural Counties Due to the Loss of Alternative Number of Producers and Secondary Workers**

| | |
|---|---|
| Under Scenario I | 976,763 |
| Under Scenario II | 1,307,688 |

[1] This represents 75.1 percent of all farms in agriculturally dependent counties in 1982. This percentage of farm failure obviously will not occur. These values illustrate, however, that the loss of farms in the most agriculturally dependent counties is likely to be very extensive and concentrated among certain types of producers and farms.
[2] Data for 1985 derived from Johnson et al. 1986.
[3] Data derived from surveys conducted by the authors in 1985, 1986 and 1987.

**Table 4.4**
**Estimated Economic and Business-Related Losses Due to the Loss of Alternative Numbers of Producers and Secondary-Worker-Related Population from Agriculturally Dependent Counties in the United States, 1985-1995**

| Item | Changes Under Alternative Scenarios[1] | |
| | Scenario I | Scenario II |
| --- | --- | --- |
| Bank deposits | $5,078,119,864 | $6,798,578,374 |
| Bank savings | 797,350,764 | 1,067,491,864 |
| S & L savings | 822,365,652 | 1,100,981,758 |
| Retail sales | $2,907,411,722 | $3,892,437,947 |
| Number of private sector business establishments | 18,930 | 25,343 |
| Total personal income | $7,630,527,256 | $10,215,737,117 |

[1]Based on 1982 per capita rates of $5,199 for bank deposits, $816 for bank savings, $842 for S & L savings, and 1979 per capita personal income of $7,812 and 1982 values of 19.38 private sector business establishments per 1,000 population.

**Table 4.5**

**Estimated Change in the Number and Proportion of Households with Poverty Incomes Due to Alternative Numbers of Producers and Secondary-Worker-Related Populations Leaving Agriculturally Dependent Counties in the United States, 1985-1995***

|  | Percent of Households in Poverty | Number of Households in Poverty |
|---|---|---|
| **Base Period (1985) After Loss of Population but Assuming No Income Effect** | | |
| Scenario I | 20.9 | 243,352 |
| Scenario II | 20.9 | 221,041 |
| **Future Dates After Assumed Loss of Population and Related Income** | | |
| Scenario I | 33.7 | 392,390 |
| Scenario II | 41.3 | 436,794 |

**Additional Households Entering Poverty Under Alternative Scenarios**

|  | Number of Additional Households | Additional Households as a Percent of All Households |
|---|---|---|
| Scenario I | 149,038 | 12.8 |
| Scenario II | 215,753 | 20.4 |

*Scenario I assumes a loss of 266,875 households and income loss of $6,143 for each remaining household, while Scenario II assumes a loss of 373,625 households and an income loss of $9,104 for each remaining household.

1982 population and economic censuses. In Table 4.4, values are in dollars for those years. The use of per capita rates is an admittedly simple means of projecting impacts and results in projected changes that are proportional to the potential changes in population (23.9 and 32.0 percent for Scenarios I and II respectively), but it nevertheless provides useful insight into the potential impacts of the crisis in agriculturally dependent areas.

Data on the general impacts of the crisis on the resource base of agriculturally dependent rural areas are presented in Table 4.4. Although it is clear that persons being forced to leave an area due to financial problems are unlikely to have the levels of savings and bank deposits assumed in the data shown in Table 4.4, it seems feasible to assume that such persons are likely to leave levels of unpaid debts at least as large as the savings noted in Table 4.4. In addition, it must be assumed that were such persons to remain in the area under "normal" financial conditions, they would eventually come to display the income characteristics of the average person in this population and thus contribute at the level of the per capita averages shown in Table 4.4.

The data in Table 4.4 suggest that the impacts on the resource base of rural areas could be substantial. The crisis could result in the loss of the equivalence of from $5 to $6 billion in bank deposits, nearly $1 billion in bank savings and an equivalent amount in savings and loan savings, and from between $7 to $10 billion in total personal income. Finally, between 18,000 and 25,000 small businesses would probably be lost due to the loss of producers and secondary workers. Such impacts are extensive and will markedly alter the resource base of such areas.

In Table 4.5 results are reported on the potential effects of the crisis on the incidence of poverty in agriculturally dependent rural counties. In this analysis, we have made several additional assumptions to discern the potential effects of the loss of producers and secondary workers and their dependents on levels of income loss and on poverty. Specifically, we have assumed that if the number of households lost were as indicated above, the income lost to the area would be equivalent to the difference between the amount of income required to maintain the households that would leave the area (which is assumed to be the amount necessary to support them at poverty levels taking into account the number of persons in the household) and the total amount of income shown in Table 4.4 as potentially being lost (i.e., $7.6 or $10.2 billion). This difference is the appropriate value to use because, if the households assumed to leave the area had remained in the area, it would have required a minimum of the poverty level of income to support them. For purposes of this analysis, these losses, which were in 1979 dollars in Table 4.4, were inflated to 1985 dollar values so that they are similar to the household income values obtained in our surveys. The income loss is assumned to be distributed equally among all remaining households. As shown in Table 4.5, this loss is $6,143 per remaining household in agriculturally dependent counties under Scenario I and $9,104 under Scenario II.

To estimate the distributional effects for the remaining households, data on the detailed distribution of income in our survey populations of producers and of other rural resident households by size of household were assumed to apply to the remaining households in agriculturally dependent counties, and the effects of the income loss on such households were examined. The effects on poverty shown in Table 4.5 were determined assuming that all persons in agriculturally dependent counties had the distributional characteristics of our survey populations (sufficiently detailed data for more representative national populations were not available).

The results in Table 4.5 show that the projected loss of households would probably result in an additional 149,038 househbolds or an additional 12.8 percent of all households living at poverty levels under Scenario I, and 215,753 additional households or an additional 20.4 percent of all households living with poverty incomes under Scenario II. Although income effects will obviously not be distributed in the proportional manner assumed, these data make it evident that the effects of the farm crisis on agriculturally dependent areas are likely to include reductions in income and increased rates of poverty for those who remain in such areas. Remaining residents will probably suffer substantial losses in the resource bases necessary to maintain their households and to maintain their communities.

## SUMMARY AND CONCLUSIONS

The analysis reported in this chapter suggests that the impacts of the farm financial crisis of the 1980s are likely to be significant for the resource bases of rural areas, particularly the most agriculturally dependent rural areas. Although the total range of impacts is unlikely to be known for years to come, it is evident that the impacts extend beyond the impacts on agricultural producers: the crisis is a rural, not only a farm, crisis. In fact, although there has been some alleviation of financial stress for selected agricultural producers as a result of aid programs, loan forgiveness, and other factors, the effects of the crisis are still evolving in the nonfarm sectors. Since such nonfarm effects are occurring in areas that are already struggling to maintain the public services and quality of life of their residents and are occurring at a time when public perceptions are that the crisis is abating, if not over, such impacts may have substantial and negative impacts and go largely unnoticed and unaddressed as vital policy concerns for rural areas.

The results in this chapter suggest that the impacts of the crisis are likely to include a loss of between 976,000 and 1,307,000 persons—between 23.9 and 32.0 percent of all persons—in agriculturally dependent counties in the United States. These losses would disproportionately include young adults and between 200,000 and 275,000 school children. The magnitude of such losses would be equivalent to the death of 600 average sized rural towns (of 800 persons in 1980). They would likely result in the direct loss of between

$7.6 and $10.2 billion in income from such areas and could result in from 149,000 to 216,000 additional households in such areas moving into income categories that are less than the 1985 level of poverty. Clearly, then, the impacts of the farm crisis on agriculturally dependent rural areas in the United States are likely to be substantial and pervasive.

These impacts have numerous implications for the development of policy for rural areas. Among the most important of these implications is the fact that the crisis is likely to lead to effects that are sufficiently large to permanently alter the viability of many rural areas. Many of these areas already have such low levels of income and services that the losses likely to result from the farm crisis will result in their having remaining population bases that are of insufficient size to support the existing businesses and services. Such areas could lose such vital commercial enterprises as clothing and furniture stores, implement dealers, hardware stores, and numerous other types of establishments for which the necessary base of population to support such services is already marginal. Equally important, for many rural hospitals and schools, enrollments and patient censuses may fall below the levels necessary to support even a minimum base of services. For yet other rural areas, services and businesses may have to be reduced to levels that are unlikely to be competitive with those in larger trading centers.

For schools in particular, it appears that in many rural areas, such as the Great Plains where enrollments per school are already small, the effects of the crisis may be to cause schools to curtail their range of offerings and services to such levels that their students will find it increasingly difficult to compete with students from other more urban schools in higher education and work settings. In fact, we maintain that among the potential implications of the crisis is the possibility that numerous additional rural areas may have their resource bases reduced to the level that the recurrent cycle of inadequate services and opportunities leading to poorly educated and thereby uncompetitive populations which experience additional economic deprivation—that is, the cycle leading to long-term poverty conditions—may be established in additional rural areas.

Equally important as the loss of physical services and material resources is the potential loss of human resources. Those leaving rural areas are likely to be young, highly educated, and innovative adults (Murdock et al. 1986). Their outmigration represents not only a numerical loss but also a loss of individuals who are among the most promising leaders of such areas for the future. As a result, the loss of such persons means that along with the lack of resources noted above, many rural areas may find that they also will no longer have the types of leaders who can assist them in developing programs to acquire new, or enhance existing, resource bases.

In sum, the impacts of the current farm crisis could result in declines in financial, service, and human resource bases in rural areas that are sufficient in magnitude to not only make such areas poorer and less desirable areas in which to live but also create conditions that are nearly irreversible.

In fact, because the present crisis is likely to impact areas that are already relatively disadvantaged, the crisis may result in many rural areas in the nation becoming areas in which the potential for new forms of development is severely limited.

It is essential, then, that policymakers become aware of the total magnitude of the impacts of the crisis for rural areas—not only of the direct impacts on agricultural producers—and that policies be developed to assist the nonagricultural as well as the agricultural sectors of rural America that are being impacted by the crisis. To delay doing so, or to fail to do so at all, appears likely to lead to conditions that will be negative and enduring. Equally important, such delays may lead to unnecessary losses in human potential and to conditions that are not only difficult but also expensive to reverse in a period of limited governmental resources.

## REFERENCES

Albrecht, D. E., and S. H. Murdock. 1987. *The Farm Crisis in Texas: Changes in the Financial Condition of Texas Farmers and Ranchers, 1985-86.* TAES Technical Report no. 87-3. College Station: Texas Agricultural Experiment Station.

Albrecht, D. E., et al. 1987. *Farm Crisis: Impact on Producers and Rural Communities in Texas.* TAES Technical Report no. 87-5. College Station: Texas Agricultural Experiment Station.

_____. *The Implications of the Farm Crisis for the Residents and Businesses of Rural Communities.* TAES Technical Report no. 88-4. College Station: Texas Agricultural Experiment Station.

Albrecht, D. E., S. H. Murdock, and R. Hamm. 1988. "The Consequencs of the Farm Crisis for Rural Communities." *Journal of the Community Development Society* 19: 119-35.

Barry, P. J. 1986. *Fiancial Stress in Agriculture: Policy and Financial Consequences.* Department of Agricultural Economics, Report no. AE4621. Champaign: University of Illinois at Urbana.

Bender, L. D., B. L. Green, T. F. Hady, J. A. Kuehn, M. K. Nelson, L. B. Perkinson, P. J. Ross, 1985. *The Diverse Social and Economic Structure of Nonmetropolitan America.* Rural Development Research Report no. 40. Economic Research Service, U.S. Dept. of Agriculture. Washington, D.C.: U.S. Government Printing Office.

Bloomquist, L. E. 1987. "Performance of the Rural Manufacturing Sectors." In *Rural Economic Development in the 1980s: Preparing for the Future.* Agriculture and Rural Economy Division, Economic Research Service, Report no. AGES870724. U.S. Department of Agriculture. Washington, D.C.: U.S. Government Printing Office.

Brown, D. L., and K. L. Deavers. 1987. "Rural Change and the Rural Economic Policy Agenda for the 1980s." In *Rural Economic Development in the 1980s: Preparing for the Future.* Agriculture and Rural Economy Division, Economic Research Service, Report no. AGES870724. U.S. Department of Agriculture. Washington, D.C.: U.S. Government Printing Office.

Bultena, G., et al. 1986. "The Farm Crisis: Patterns and Impacts of Financial

Distress among Iowa Farm Families." *Rural Sociology* 51(4): 436-48.

Deavers, K. L., Robert A. Hoppe, and Peggy J. Ross. 1986. "Public Policy and Rural Poverty: A View from the 1980s." *Policy Studies Journal* 15(2): 291-309.

Doeksen, G. A. 1987. "The Agricultural Crisis As It Affects Rural Communities." *Journal of the Community Development Society* 18(1): 78-88.

Doeksen, G. A., and J. Peterson. 1987. *Critical Issues in the Delivery of Local Government Services in Rural America.* Agriculture and Rural Economics Division, Economic Research Service, Staff Report AGES860917. U.S. Department of Agriculture. Washington, D.C.: U.S. Government Printing Office.

Dunn, J. C. 1987. "Rural Farm Population Loss: Economic and Demographic Implications for North Dakota's State Planning, Region 6." Master's thesis, North Dakota State University, Fargo.

Engels, R. A. 1986. "The Metropolitan/Nonmetropolitan Population at Mid-Decade." Paper presented at the annual meeting of the Population Association of America, San Francisco.

Fuguitt, G. V. 1985. "The Nonmetropolitan Population Turnaround." *Annual Review of Sociology* 11: 259-80.

Ginder, R. G. 1985. *The Structure of Production Agriculture and the Farm Debt Crisis.* Ames: Iowa State University.

Goreham, G. A., et al. 1987. "Implications of Trade and Market Patterns of North Dakota Farm and Ranch Operators." *North Dakota Farm Research* 44(4): 23-27.

Heffernan, J. B., and W. D. Heffernan. 1985. *The Effects of the Agricultural Crisis on the Health and Lives of Farm Families.* Columbia: University of Missouri.

Henry, M., et al. 1986. "A Changing Rural America." *Economic Review* 71: 23-41.

Johnson, J., et al. 1987. *Financial Characteristics of U.S. Farms, January 1, 1987.* Economic Research Service, Agricultural Information Bulletin no. 525. U.S. Department of Agriculture. Washington, D.C.: U.S. Government Printing Office.

———. 1986. *Financial Characteristics of U.S. Farms, January 1, 1986.* Economic Research Service, Agricultural Information Bulletin no. 500. U.S. Department of Agriculture. Washington, D.C.: U.S. Government Printing Office.

———. 1985. *Financial Characteristics of U.S. Farms, 1985.* Economic Research Service, Agricultural Information Bulletin no. 495. U.S. Department of Agriculture. Washington, D.C.: U.S. Government Printing Office.

Johnson, J. D., et al. 1984. "Financial Conditions of the Farm Sector and Farm Operators." *Agricultural Finance Review* 47: 1-18.

Johnson, K. M. 1985. *The Impact of Population Change on Business Activity in Rural America.* Boulder, Colo.: Westview Press.

Korsching, P. F., and J. Gildner, eds. 1986. *Interdependencies of Agriculture and Rural Communities in the Twenty-First Century: The North Central Region Conference Proceedings.* Ames: The North Central Regional Center for Rural Development, Iowa State University.

Leholm, A. G., et al. 1985. *Selected Financial and Other Socioeconomic Characteristics of North Dakota Farm and Ranch Operators.* Ag. Eco. Report no. 199. Fargo: North Dakota State University.

Long, R. W., et al. 1987. *Rural Policy Formulation in the United States.* Agriculture and Rural Economics Division, Economic Research Service, Staff Report no. AGES870203. U.S. Department of Agriculture. Washington, D.C.: U.S. Government Printing Office.

Marousek, G. 1979. "Farm Size and Rural Communities: Some Economic Relationships." *Southern Journal of Agricultural Economics* 2(2): 61-65.

Morrissey, E. S. 1985. *Characteristics of Poverty in Nonmetro Counties.* Economic Development Division, Economic Research Service, Rural Development Research Report no. 52. U.S. Department of Agriculture. Washington, D.C.: U.S. Government Printing Office.

Murdock, S. H., and F. L. Leistritz. 1988. *The Farm Financial Crisis: Socioeconomic Dimensions and Implications for Producers and Rural Areas.* Boulder, Colo.: Westview Press.

Murdock, S. H., et al. 1985. *The Farm Crisis in Texas: An Examination of the Characteristics of Farmers and Ranchers under Financial Stress in Texas.* Department of Rural Sociology Technical Report 85-2. College Station: Texas Agricultural Experiment Station.

_____. 1987. "Impacts of the Farm Crisis on a Rural Community." *Journal of the Community Development Society* 18(1): 30-49.

_____. 1988. "The Implications of the Current Farm Crisis for Rural America." In *The Farm Financial Crisis: Socioeconomic Dimensions and Implications for Producers and Rural Areas.* Boulder, Colo.: Westview Press.

_____. 1986. "The State of Socioeconomic Impact Analysis in the United States: Limitations and Opportunities for Alternative Futures." *Journal of Environmental Management* 23: 99-117.

Popovich, M. G. 1987. *State Emergency Farm Finance.* Vol. 2. Washington, D.C.: Council of State Policy and Planning Agencies.

Reimund, D., and M. Petrulis. 1987. "Performance of the agricultural sector." In *Rural Economic Development in the 1980s: Preparing for the Future.* Agriculture and Rural Economy Division, Economic Research Service, Report no. AGES870724. U.S. Department of Agriculture. Washington, D.C.: U.S. Government Printing Office.

Richter, K. 1985. "Nonmetropolitan Growth in the Late 1970s: The End of the Turnaround?" *Demography* 22: 245-63.

Stinson, J., et al. 1986. *Governing the Heartlands: Can Rural Communities Survive the Farm Crisis?* A report prepared for the Senate Subcommittee on Intergovernmental Relations. Washington, D.C.: U.S. Congress.

# 5
# Rural Poverty, Welfare Eligibility, Farm Programs, and the Negative Income Tax

## DAVID L. DEBERTIN and CRAIG L. INFANGER

The rural poverty problem in the United States is complex and multifaceted. In some regions, rural poverty has been widespread and chronic over several generations, leading to difficult long-term social problems. In other areas, rural poverty has more recently arisen as a result of the financial crisis that has greatly affected agriculture during the 1980s and the industrial transition affecting the textile and other manufacturing businesses located in nonmetropolitan counties. This transition has left some farm and rural families—many who were only recently earning incomes well above the poverty level—with serious economic problems (Drabenstott 1986; Rodgers and Weiher 1986).

Just as the causes of rural poverty are multifaceted, so are the strategies for alleviating rural poverty. Strategies for alleviating rural poverty can be broadly classified into four different categories. A simple means of eliminating rural poverty is for the federal government to provide income support payments to all individuals whose incomes fall below a certain predetermined poverty level. Presumably, the same income support program could be used for both rural and urban residents. However, such a strategy represents only a symptomatic treatment of the rural poverty problem. If no other steps are taken, payments to individuals below the poverty level would need to continue indefinitely, with consequent implications for taxpayers.

A second strategy involves upgrading educational levels and/or the specific job skills of those rural residents who are in poverty. In many areas, where the percentage of individuals classified as rural poor is high, the average educational level is low, and a high percentage of individuals never completed high school. In eastern Kentucky, for example, many of the high schools continue to be plagued with very high dropout rates. Limitations in specific employable job skills among those in poverty also pose a problem. From a policy-making perspective, it is often unclear whether scarce tax dollars should be allocated to basic educational programs aimed at older residents who never completed high school and are in poverty, programs designed to reduce dropout rates among school-age children, vocational programs for school-age children, vocational programs for developing and upgrading employable skills among those who are already in poverty, or some combination of these options.

Rural economic development programs designed to bring light industry to small rural communities can also be thought of as a strategy for dealing with rural poverty. This strategy may, at first, be thought of as primarily beneficial to rural nonfarm residents. Increasingly, however, farmers with inadequate earnings from the farm also hold part-time off-farm jobs in manufacturing. This is particularly true in a state such as Kentucky, where the average farm size is only approximately 150 acres, and income from a hypothetical average farm often is not sufficient to provide an adequate income to support a family. Part-time off-farm employment is clearly more feasible in a rural area in which the local community has been able to attract light industry. Alleviating rural poverty, in part, involves understanding what factors influence a manufacturer to locate a plant in a rural area. Empirical research has been conducted to identify factors affecting locational decisions by firms seeking to locate in rural areas (Smith, Deaton, and Kelch 1978).

Federal farm policy has an impact on the rural poverty problem. U.S. farm policy has served a number of objectives, some of which have had an impact on incomes of farmers and on rural poverty. However, the primary objectives of government farm policy have been more closely linked to attempting to maintain a structure of agriculture consisting largely of family farms and to ensure a low-cost, stable food supply for consumers. If the needs of the rural poor were served as the primary objectives were met, so much the better. However, while the stated general goal of politicians who make federal farm policy has been to attempt to preserve a structure largely consisting of family farms, farm policy at the federal level has never been specifically directed toward improving the well-being of low-income farmers, at least not as a primary objective.

In this chapter, four paradigms of rural poverty are developed. These paradigms were designed to explain how different factors interact and result in significant numbers of rural poor—poverty that persists even though the national economy has experienced sustained economic growth for over six consecutive years. Some of the factors involved in the persistence of rural poverty are partially or even totally under the control of the individual in poverty. However, in recent years, many of the factors leading to rural poverty have arisen as a result of events in the U.S. macroeconomy and in world economies affecting agriculture.

In the remainder of this chapter, these policy alternatives for dealing with the rural poverty problem are further developed. Focus is placed on the impacts of government policy for food and agriculture as tools for alleviating rural poverty, and on strategies involving economic development within rural areas. Strategies involving changes in welfare programs are also addressed. Consequences of each of these policy alternatives follow from the rural poverty paradigms. Although implementation of these policy alternatives is usually thought of primarily as a responsibility of policymakers at the federal level, in some instances, units of state and local government, as well as decision makers within the private sectors (including organizations and leadership within small rural communities) may also have responsibilities.

## LINKING CAUSES AND SOLUTIONS: THE PARADIGMS OF RURAL POVERTY

The multifaceted nature of the rural poverty problem in the United States suggests that no single model or paradigm of rural poverty will adequately describe the problem. Thus, we proceed by first defining four categories of rural poverty and then developing a paradigm for each category. These four paradigms establish the basic linkages among the factors that lead to rural poverty and provide insights into possible policy prescriptions.

### Traditional Rural Poverty: The Farm Sector

Nearly every state and region of the country has places where rural poverty among farmers has been widespread for a number of generations. For example, large pockets of rural poverty are commonplace in Appalachia and the Southeast. In these sparsely populated counties, farming is an important source of income, but per capita incomes average only 70 percent of incomes in all nonmetropolitan counties (Bender et al. 1985). These "persistent poverty counties" are called here *traditional rural poverty in the farm sector*. Traditional rural poverty among those engaged directly in agricultural production leads to what is sometimes termed subsistence agriculture, or subsistence farming. A key characteristic of these farmers is that they have only limited access to credit markets, making expansion of the farm to improve income difficult.

Figure 5.1 is a paradigm of *traditional rural poverty within the farming*

**Figure 5.1**
**Paradigm of Traditional Poverty: The Farm Sector**

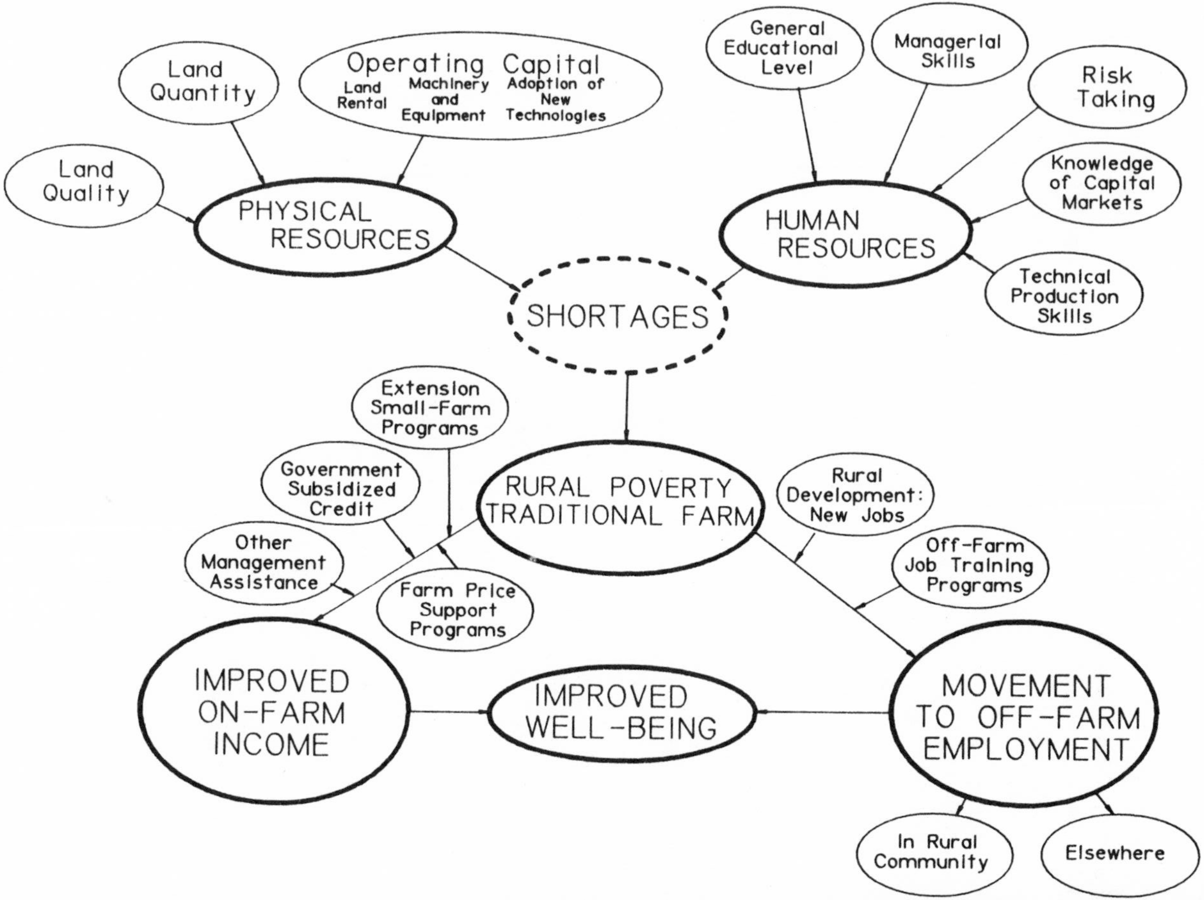

*sector*. An important characteristic of this group of farmers is that the poverty persists irrespective of what the specifics of federal farm programs or the general well-being of the larger, commercial farmers might be at any particular point in time. These subsistence farmers have received poverty-level incomes in periods of low farm prices and high farm prices, in periods when the government was providng substantial price and income support, and in periods when farm prices and incomes were largely determined by the free market. However, the recent period of extraordinarily low farm prices may have made economic conditions even worse for these farmers and served to highlight the problems of this group.

The basic cause of this poverty is that resources owned by these farmers are insufficient, in most years, to provide an acceptable standard of living. As suggested by Figure 5.1, these resources might be *physical* resources such as land or capital equipment used in agricultural production. Frequently, these farms are located in regions where the climate, land slope, or soil conditions are only marginally suited to agricultural production. Access to capital needed to rent or purchase additional land, improve soil fertility, or adopt new technologies imposes a significant constraint.

U.S. farmers have sometimes been thought of as being on a "technology treadmill." A new production technology is developed through either publicly or privately funded agricultural research. The new technology is usually not secret. Information about technologies developed with public funds are available to any farmer. Private firms engaged in agricultural research are generally interested in making money from the new technologies they develop. Examples of new agricultural technologies developed with private sector funding include improved corn varieties, a new pesticide, or an improved piece of farm machinery.

The actual adoption of a new technology (from publicly or privately funded research), whether it be new varieties of crops, fertilization programs, pesticides, or new labor-saving machinery and equipment, nearly always requires a significant capital investment. By virtue of the fact that some farmers have better access to capital to purchase new technologies than others, some farmers have access to the new technology earlier than others. These farmers often can produce a commodity at a lower cost than those who had insufficient capital to adopt the new technology.

Assuming that the new technology is able to reduce per-unit production costs, in order to remain competitive, other farmers must eventually use the new technology, or they will not be cost competitive per unit of grain or livestock product produced, and they will eventually go out of business. The farm is sold to a neighboring farmer who is able to adopt the technology and is cost competitive. Many of the farmers without sufficient capital needed to upgrade continously their agricultural production technologies eventually end up in rural poverty.

Alternately or in addition, the resource in short supply might be the *human* resource, viewed in productivity terms as "human capital." The human resource shortages might be measured not only by the amount of formal education, but also other specific skills used in earning a livng on the farm. Farmers in this category often not only lack access to capital markets needed to obtain new technologies, but they also lack technical production and needed financial management skills. Technical production skills could be measured by comparing, for example, the farmer's crop yields with crop yields on other, neighboring farms with similar land quality and weather conditions.

Farmers at or near the poverty level face difficult choices when making financial decisions. Income earned from the farm could be used to upgrade the standard of living for the family, or it could be reinvested in the farm in an effort to improve productivity and income one or more years hence. In reality, all farmers face allocation decisions in the use of income for family living expenses versus reinvestment in the farm. But for farmers at or near the poverty level, it becomes far more difficult to make the decision to reinvest income. This is despite the fact that reinvestment rather than consumption may be critical for getting the farmer above the poverty level over a longer period of time.

Those in this category are only marginally affected by what the federal government does with respect to specific farm programs for agriculture. To the extent that farm programs increase incomes of all farmers who produce a particular commodity and participate in the program, those in this category may also benefit proportionally to the amount of the commodity produced.

### Traditional Rural Poverty: The Nonfarm Sector

One characteristic of a rural community is that those not directly engaged in farming rely heavily on farmers and farming—either directly or indirectly—as a primary source of income. Rural towns contain businesses, which primarily serve farmers as suppliers of inputs or as purchasers of grain and livestock from farmers. In rural communities that lack manufacturing jobs, the impact of agriculture on nonfarm employment can be very important.

In rural areas where there is limited employment in other industries (such as manufacturing or mining) and a subsistence agriculture dominates, there is likely to be considerable poverty in the nonfarm sector as well. Furthermore, difficulties in manufacturing and energy industries can exacerbate poverty problems arising from weaknesses within the farm economy. In eastern Kentucky, for example, the downturn in coal prices closely coincided with the downturn in prices for key agricultural commodities, making the situation even more difficult for rural residents.

Figure 5.2 is a paradigm of *traditional poverty in the rural nonfarm*

**Figure 5.2**
**Paradigm of Traditional Poverty: The Nonfarm Sector**

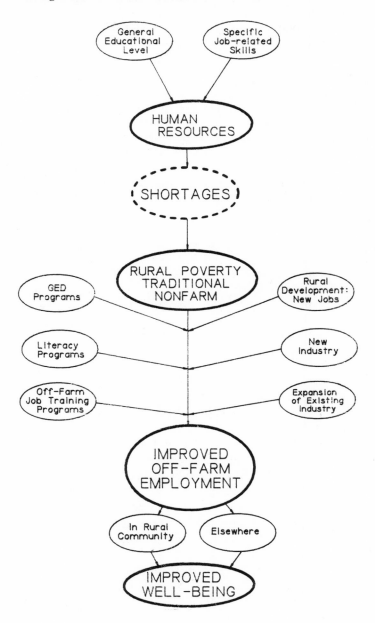

*sector.* This form of rural poverty is caused primarily by a lack of education or specific job skills since few individuals in the nonfarm sector have resources other than their own skills to market. Among those in the rural nonfarm sector are those who have low formal education levels, and those who lack specific skills needed for employment within the rural community. Even for those with specific employable skills, job opportunities for skilled workers may be limited, unless the individual is willing to relocate to another community where these skills are in greater demand.

High unemployment is characteristic of those in this classification. Many of the employed individuals may be earning minimum wage or less. In other instances, employment might be for only part of the year. In Kentucky, for example, many rural residents survive primarily on the seasonal employment provided with the production, marketing, and harvesting of tobacco.

This category of rural poor is little affected by what happens with respect to federal farm price support programs for agricultural commodities, or with the general state of the agricultural economy. If the agricultural economy is prosperous, there might be more opportunities for employment within the rural community, and, therefore, to a limited degree, those in this category may be better off with a booming, rather than a weak, farm economy. The basic problem, however, remains. Within the rural community, the skills of the individuals who fall into this category are not sufficiently in demand to provide more than poverty-level incomes.

Alleviating poverty among those in this category of rural poor involves strategies by policymakers both in education and economic development. First, more efforts could be directed at upgrading the specific human resource skills that are deficient. If a lack of literacy is an obstacle to employment in higher paying jobs, then specific efforts in some states and regions need to be directed toward pushing literacy programs. These efforts might be combined with or added to efforts aimed at achieving the equivalent of a high school diploma.

In other instances, it is not the general educational level that poses a barrier so much as a lack of specific employable skills. Here vocational colleges and other programs specifically directed toward providing specific skills for employment can be important.

Upgrading the skills of these individuals is not going to solve the problem if few job opportunities exist within the rural communities once the skills are upgraded. The second strategy involves efforts on the part of the rural community to provide new (presumably higher paying) jobs within the local community. This generally involves attracting new firms to the community or expanding employment opportunities within existing firms.

Rural communities are frequently unsuccessful in their attempts to attract new firms. There are thousands of other rural communities in the United States also in search of industrial development. To the firm seeking a plant site, many of these communities may appear to possess very similar characteristics. A competition among the communities ensues, involving tax breaks and special incentives to attract a firm. Competition among small communities who seek a plant may ultimately prove destructive. Tax breaks and other special incentives needed in order to attract a new plant may be more costly than the benefits derived from new jobs in the plant. Competition among various states for new automobile assembly plants resulted in tax breaks and other special incentives to firms that in some instances exceeded the economic benefits to the state from the plants. Similar competitions among rural communities can lead to results that are not ultimately beneficial to the community.

However, if off-farm job opportunities are not available within the rural communities, those workers with specific skills willing to bear the relocation costs will relocate into communities where the skills are employable, leaving behind the rural community in as bad a shape as before. Programs aimed at upgrading job skills and rural industrialization programs must both be successful if those in this category are to be helped.

### Nontraditional Rural Poverty: The Farm Sector

The farm crisis of the 1980s has had substantial impacts on net farm income. Farmers in the category labeled *nontraditional rural poverty* are those that were not in poverty prior to 1980 but were seriously hurt by the events that have taken place within the macro and farm economy since then. Analysis of farm income data from this period indicate that 15 percent of farm households had negative total income (from all sources) and an additional 18 percent had total incomes below the poverty level (Reimund and Petrulis 1987). The paradigm presented in Figure 5.3 applies to this category. There are a few similarities with Figure 5.1, but also many differences. Unlike their traditionally poor counterparts, farmers in this category had access to land and other physical inputs, which, in better times (prior to 1980), were sufficient to provide an income above the poverty level.

The human resources also differ from those shown in Figure 5.1. Generally, these farmers are well educated and possess the requisite technical skills to produce crops and livestock efficiently. If those in the traditionally poor category were often unwilling to take on risk in order to perhaps achieve a higher income, this group of farmers was perhaps too willing to take on risk in the 1980s. They were perhaps overly willing to borrow money and expand the farming operation under the implicit assumption that farm prices (and land prices) would continue increasing as they had done in the late 1970s.

There is some debate among agricultural economists with respect to the other human resource characteristics of these farmers. One view holds that the farmers who are in this category possessed inferior financial and managerial skills, or they would not have gotten themselves into such serious

Figure 5.3
Paradigm of Nontraditional Poverty: The Farm Sector

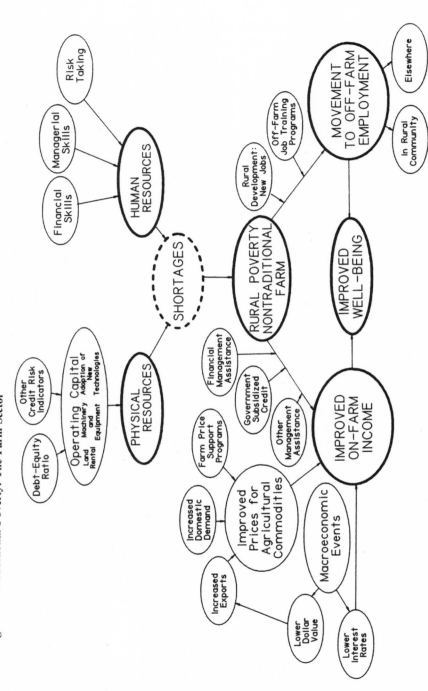

financial trouble. Another view argues that the macroeconomic and other events occurring during the 1980s were so unique that no one, not even an excellent farm manager, could have foreseen what actually happened. Therefore, these farmers now find themselves with poverty-level incomes because of a series of macroeconomic events and policy decisions by the federal government. Thus, these farmers were the victims of a situation outside their own control.

Through most of the 1970s, the general agricultural economy was booming. Prices for most agricultural commodities were high, and land values soared. There was a widespread feeling within the agricultural community that these extraordinarily good conditions were a permanent, rather than a temporary, phenomenon. To illustrate, the Secretary of Agriculture was encouraging farmers to plant crops "fence row to fence row." Agricultural exports were high, as grain deals were struck with the Soviets and many other foreign countries. Inflation was high, but increases in farmland values in most years far outdistanced inflation rates. Until the later 1970s, interest rates were well below the inflation rate for land values.

Farmers used cheap credit as a means of expanding the size of their operation. High net worths were achieved through leverage—using borrowed funds to continue to expand. Agricultural creditors were unconcerned about the credit expansion because they "knew" that, within a year, the land purchased on credit would be worth far more than its current price. The primary criterion for the extension of additional credit to the farmer was the value of the farmland already owned, not the income stream from the production of crops and livestock.

Starting in the late 1970s, conditions changed dramatically. The Federal Reserve decided that inflation rates exceeding 10 percent were unacceptable and attempted to bring down inflation by restricting the money supply. This meant higher interest rates. The U.S. economy went into a massive recession just as many of the export markets for agricultural commodities dried up.

Domestic consumption of the major agricultural commodities grows slowly from year to year. Variation in export demand largely determines the price level. President Carter decided for political reasons he no longer wanted to sell grain to the Soviets. Arab nations were heavily subsidizing grain production and irrigation projects in their own countries. Production of major agricultural commodities by members of the European Economic Community also increased substantially. Even India became a net exporter of certain grains. The U.S. export market for grains deteriorated, resulting in substantial decreases in prices for most major crops.

The decreases in crop prices resulted in severe cash flow problems for many farmers. Meanwhile, interest rates were increasing on the credit previously extended to farmers. Many farmers faced greater and greater demands for cash to service debt taken on in better times. As crop prices decreased and fewer farmers had funds to purchase land, land values dropped. Creditors were faced with situations where land values were often no longer high enough to cover loans even as the farmer's capacity for repaying the debt deteriorated and crop prices declined. Many farmers made valiant attempts to continue, but bankruptcy was frequently the only solution.

It was particularly the farmers who expanded during the late 1970s on borrowed capital who got into serious financial difficulty as prices for agricultural commodities decreased and interest rates remained high. Farmers who found themselves in this situation in many instances made every effort to hold on to the farmland. Making payments on interest and debt frequently involved making drastic cuts in family living expenses. While some of these farmers continued to have a positive net worth, they and their families in many instances were living at the poverty level—without access to the "social safety net" available to nonfarm residents living on poverty-level incomes and without other assets. The financial difficulties faced by these farmers were and often continue to be very severe.

In comparison with the farmers labeled as traditionally poor, this group of farmers has some important advantages in dealing with their income problems. Many of the farmers who overexpanded in the late 1970s had only recently begun farming—thus many are younger than those labeled as traditionally poor. They often are also better educated and, since they are younger, perhaps more open to the possibility of nonfarm employment, even if employment could only be found outside the rural community.

These farmers should benefit greatly by any improvements in the overall farm economy, whether these improvements are due to improved farm prices because of improved exports, decreases in interest rates, or government payments. Thus, the poverty may be more nearly temporary than permanent if the agricultural economy is restored to health. Other forms of assistance might also be warranted. The Farmer's Home Administration (FmHA) has traditionally been the lender to farmers ineligible for other sources of credit, and it has an obligation to ensure that their borrowers have sufficient money to cover ordinary family living expenses as well as operating expense, debt, and interest repayment. Because of the linkages between farm and family living expenses, there is no way the FmHA can avoid getting involved in family finances. The FmHA has always provided managerial assistance in conjunction with the credit.

The agricultural extension service has had a long record of providing management assistance to farmers. During the past five years, the focus of much of these efforts has been directed toward financial management with emphasis on financial record keeping and the use of financial records for decision making.

Farmers in financial difficulty who had the opportunity and specific skills frequently have been taking employment part-time off-farm. In other instances, the spouse has taken full-time off-farm employment. Off-farm employment can be a very effective survival strategy, particularly if problems within the agricultural economy are viewed as short term. But the strategy is dependent on the availability of jobs within the community, and some communities are better positioned to provide these jobs than others. Finally, the solution for some of the farmers who fall into this category in dealing with their income problems is in finding permanent off-farm employment.

Bruce Jones and William Heffernan (1987) have called for a government loan program specifically to meet the needs of exiting farmers. Such a program would make transition loans available to farmers at low interest rates until they could systematically liquidate remaining assets and perhaps obtain off-farm employment. Exiting farmers, having made every effort to save the farm, frequently find themselves in a precarious financial situation with respect to meeting even necessary family living expenses. It may be necessary for the federal government to guarantee loans, given the debt/equity situation faced by the exiting farmers. Eligibility requirements for loan funds would need to be developed, repayment plans and strategies discussed, and participating credit institutions identified. Ideally, loans should be paid off as the exiting farmers find new employment and the need for the financial assistance is reduced.

The cost of this kind of program could be quite high, particularly if exiting farmers are not successful at finding off-farm work, as the number of exiting farmers increases. Moreover, if the government-guaranteed loans are defaulted, costs could increase quite rapidly.

### Nontraditional Rural Poverty: The Nonfarm Sector

Figure 5.4 is a paradigm of *nontraditional rural poverty within the nonfarm sector*. Traditional nonfarm rural poverty occurs primarily because of deficiencies in education and job skills and a lack of job opportunities within the rural community. In contrast, nontraditional poverty within the nonfarm sector is closely linked to events that have taken place within the farm sector and the macro economy.

Businesses in rural communities are closely tied to the general health of agriculture, particularly in those communities that lack other industrial and energy-related places of employment (Stone 1987). Those who work for businesses that serve farmers in recent years have faced very difficult times, leading to low incomes, perhaps at the poverty level. Unemployment insurance as well as social welfare programs should be available to these people.

The role of the rural community in serving the needs of residents in the rural area is being restructured. This is not a recent change, but it has been occurring for a long period of time. In horse and buggy days, rural communities needed to be located within a few miles of the farmers in order to make it possible for farmers to obtain supplies without having to travel long

**Figure 5.4**
**Paradigm of Nontraditional Poverty: The Nonfarm Sector**

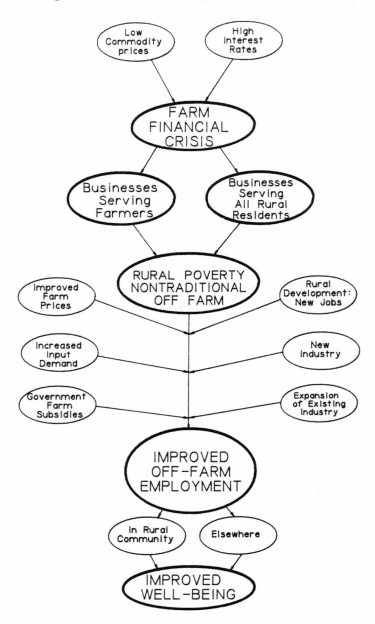

distances. As transportation systems improved, it became possible for rural residents to travel longer distances to obtain goods and services, and the need for many small rural communities declined.

As a result, over time, many small rural communities experienced a loss of population and businesses. Consequently, there are often businesses in small rural communities that are on the verge of being abandoned, as structural changes continue. Low, even poverty-level, incomes can result for the individuals who operate these businesses and their (perhaps former) employees. The loss of a local business may not necessarily result in more rural poverty if the former owners and employees have other employable skills and other job opportunities. Frequently, however, those no longer employed must leave the community to find work, and, as people leave the community, it becomes more and more difficult for the businesses that remain to continue in operation. A cycle that could lead to continuing rural poverty in the nonfarm sector persists.

Aside from industrial development efforts, there is little that policy-makers can do to affect the structural changes now taking place in many of the small rural communities. Many rural areas probably have more small communities than are needed in order to provide essential goods and services. Businesses such as grocery stores and filling stations can usually survive in small towns, but rural residents often seek larger towns and cities in order to purchase goods such as clothing and furniture. Main street businesses in small rural towns must compete with discount stores located twenty or thirty miles away and may be at a competitive disadvantage in price as well as selection.

Of course, for many rural communities, agriculture is the primary employer and source of wealth. Secondary and tertiary employment and income are closely tied to the overall health of the agricultural sector. As a result, programs directed toward improving the general farm economy should also aid the nonfarm sector within rural communities. This is true not only for the farm machinery dealers and the fertilizer and pesticide dealers, but also for businesses such as hardware, clothing, grocery stores, and restaurants. A general improvement in the farm economy should also result in income improvements for this group of individuals. Job opportunities less tied to the health of the farm economy could also be beneficial. This involves rural development efforts similar to those discussed earlier.

## POLICY STRATEGIES

### Welfare Programs for the Rural Poor

Fewer of the rural poor who live on farms are eligible for welfare and other forms of government assistance than most of the urban poor with similar incomes. This happens because many of the rural poor who live on farms, despite having very low (perhaps even negative) incomes, still have a positive net worth, with most of the net worth in farmland and other assets of value such as farm machinery and equipment used to operate the farm. Farms with a negative net worth are technically insolvent, and are, or will shortly be, in bankruptcy proceedings.

For most public assistance programs, eligibility for assistance is determined in part not only by current income, but also the value of owned assets. Thus, perhaps a majority of the rural poor who still live on farms and own farmland would be ineligible for public assistance in that, even though they may be near bankruptcy, they are not quite insolvent. If these people wish to obtain public assistance, they would be forced to sell farmland and other assets of value, use any proceeds for family living expenses for a time, and then, if their income was low enough, finally meet the criteria for public assistance as applied to rural nonfarm and urban dwellers.

Despite the harsh economic conditions, the rural poor who live on farms are frequently reluctant to sacrifice their way of life and leave the farm in order to become eligible for government income assistance if there is any prospect for continuing. However, continuing to farm requires that these low-income farmers retain to the maximum extent possible the assets used in farming, and the value of these assets frequently renders them ineligible for many forms of public assistance that would be available to the urban poor with similar incomes. The value of these assets in certain instances makes some of these farmers appear to be comparatively wealthy based on the standards normally applied to the urban poor, despite the very low incomes.

### Government Farm Programs as Assistance

Federal farm programs have evolved into a system in which most programs are open to producers on a year-to-year elective basis with minimal eligibility criteria. Furthermore, for many of the programs sponsored by the U.S. Department of Agriculture, payments received by farmers come in a variety of different forms. For example, direct payments are made to farmers under the target price/deficiency payment systems for crops like corn and wheat; indirect payments are received through the non-recourse price support loans when farmers default on the loan and the U.S. Department of Agriculture takes possession of the crop; indirect payments are also made through government purchases of commodities at higher-than-market prices, such as the dairy support program; and indirect benefits go to farmers whose commodities are subject to allotments or marketing quotas (e.g., tobacco and peanuts), which make resulting crop prices higher than the free market would provide.

American farmers are sometimes said to "farm the farm programs" by pursuing production decisions that maximize government payments. This behavior includes reorganizing farm ownership and tenancy to avoid the current $50,000 per person limitation on deficiency payments and the $250,000 limitation on all payments. Schemes that limit or otherwise direct farm program payments may induce farmers to pursue new avoidance behavior, and, as a result, unintended consequences for policymakers may occur.

The rules under which payments are made within the current farm legislation basically are structured such that generally the farms that are the largest and the most technologically efficient and have the best quality land and other resources receive the most benefits. Two important criteria for major commodity program benefits are (1) the acreage allotment for the eligible commodity or commodities and (2) historical yields. The farmers with the largest acreage allotments are usually those with the most land. The farmers with the largest historical yields are usually those who are the most technologically efficient or who have the farms that are endowed with the best farmland and other resources or the farms that in the historical period upon which the yields were based happened to have extraordinarily good weather. The short-run impacts of either very good or very bad weather on historical yields can be mitigated somewhat by calculating historical yields over a longer base period. However, because of these rules, the farmers who are potentially most in need of income assistance obtain the smallest benefits, and those potentially least in need receive the greatest benefits. This is opposite from the rules that generally apply to welfare and other public assistance programs in the nonfarm sector.

As a result, the belief is widespread among agricultural economists (including many of those directly involved in agricultural policy), politicians, farmers, and the public that the bulk of the benefits of farm program legislation go to large, wealthy farmers who are not truly in need of assistance (see the discussion in Pasour 1986). Some research evidence, however, now disputes this belief. A survey for the U.S. Department of Agriculture (conducted by Johnson and Banker 1987) concluded that it was the mid-size, commercial, family farms that reap the greatest share of the benefits. This study concluded that, compared to their contribution to production, neither the large "mega" farms producing more than $500,000 of output, nor the part-time and subsistence farms individually producing less than $40,000 of output receive revenues from farm programs proportionate with their contribution to output.

That neither the very small nor the very large producers benefited proportionately from government payments is not necessarily bad, if the government desires to provide the greatest assistance through government programs to farmers who truly need help. A large proportion of the middle group of farmers, those producing over $40,000 but less than $500,000 of output, were farmers with high debt loads, negative cash flows, or both. Those producing more than $500,000 of output were frequently producing commodities ineligible for government price support payments. Those producing less than $40,000 of output usually fall into either of two categories: part-time farmers with substantial off-farm income or elderly and subsistence farmers, who, while perhaps not having high total incomes, can be comparatively debt free and can have comparatively high net worths, at least relative to their incomes.

The U.S. Department of Agriculture study found that government payments went to all types of farms, regardless of their cash flow and debt situation. However, nearly 60 percent of the outlays went to farms with a high debt-to-asset ratio, negative cash flows, or both. The remaining 40 percent went to farms that were categorized as low debt and positive cash flow. E. C. Pasour, Jr., indicated that, in 1984, one-third of all government payments go to farmers who sell more than $250,000 of output. Farm programs that attempt to deal with the financial crisis within agriculture by making government payments to farmers who meet the existing eligibility requirements without reference to farmers' income or debt do little to alleviate the rural poverty problem.

Farm-state senators are increasingly becoming sensitized to the argument that the benefits of farm program legislation do not always go to the farmers who need them the most. While the U.S. Department of Agriculture study suggests that more of the benefits of farm programs do go to farmers who are in need than had been previously believed, federal farm program payments are still not made on the basis of individual farmer's needs.

Political support for payments to farmers within farm programs is generated primarily on the basis of arguments by farm-state politicians designed to create sympathy for farmers on the part of urban dwellers and politicians from urban districts. These arguments frequently leave the impression that the entire agricultural sector, including virtually all farmers, is currently facing economic hardship. Although many farmers are currently experiencing severe economic hardship, this is simply not the case for all farmers, some are doing quite well in the current economic environment.

Those farmers in greatest financial need could be identified by setting up cash flow, net worth, or income criteria for eligibility and then building these criteria into existing farm programs. Given the emphasis in the last several years on reducing federal expenditures as a means of reducing the budget deficit and the amount of public interest in the farm financial crisis, it is somewhat surprising that more questions have not been raised regarding the development of income, cash flow, or net worth criteria for eligibility for government farm payments.

Stiff eligibility requirements have the potential of saving the federal government billions of dollars and simultaneously making assistance more generous for those farmers who truly have financial problems. Yet the public and the Congress have been content to continue to make payments to farmers without regard to need. Imposing maximum income or net worth criteria for eligibilty would almost assuredly be politically unpopular with the farm leadership. One of the basic determinants of eligibility under the current wheat and feed grain programs is the willingness of the farmer to restrict production consistent with the rules that apply within the existing legislation.

Local Agricultural Conservation and Stabilization Service (ASCS) offices already collect a considerable amount of data about individual farmer's operations on historical acreages, yields, and so on in order to determine eligibility under the current legislation, but very little of this is financial data. While the profitability of the farm might be inferred on the basis of some of these data, such as yields and acreages, the legislation (and hence ASCS offices) has never required net worth, cash flow, or income statements. Such an option would require little additional work for farmers who already prepare and supply these statements to their creditors.

But there are major difficulties with this approach. If farms with positive cash flows and low debts were determined ineligible for government payments, the government might not have any effective means of restricting production on these ineligible farms. This, in turn, might mean greater output from these nonparticipating farmers and lower domestic market prices, resulting in higher government payments to the eligible farmers. Some of the savings generated by not making payments to ineligible farms would thus be offset by higher payment costs to farmers ruled eligible.

If only farmers with net worths or incomes below predetermined levels were allowed to receive government payments, the federal government would be, in effect, rewarding many farmers for inefficiency in production or an inability to manage their farms, while making it more difficult for the efficient, well-managed producers to survive. This is counter to free-enterprise principles leading to the survival of the well-managed farms and designed to promote efficiency in agricultural production.

### Rethinking Public Assistance Programs

There seems to be a growing awareness among politicians of the need to rethink the entire approach to public assistance programs in both the farm and the nonfarm sectors. Except for administrative costs, nearly all of the $23 billion spent last year for government farm programs eventually is income to farmers. Realistically, the federal government will always be involved in programs that raise the incomes of low-income people, regardless of where they reside, and the political questions are primarily the extent to which the government is involved and the mechanisms (in effect, criteria) for the distribution of these income enhancement payments. The criteria for eligibility within these programs should not exclude any particular class of low-income people by virtue of how their income is earned—either from farming or from other employment.

The current welfare and other public assistance programs primarily designed with the support of urban legislators within the individual states and urban congressmen at the federal level, usually involve eligibility requirements including not only income, but also the value of owned assets and need criteria such as the number of family members. The urban poor and, to a much lesser degree, the rural nonfarm poor, is the constituency for which most public assistance legislation is written.

Federal farm programs were written by farm-state senators and representatives in response to the articulated needs of their constituency, largely commercial farmers, commodity groups, and agribusinesses. Such legislation does not include eligibility requirements such as income, the value of owned assets, or famiy size. These farm-state senators and representatives are obviously not opposed to the fact that government farm programs will, at least to a degree, provide income assistance to low-income farmers, but this benefit is more nearly viewed a by-product of the legislation than a major objective.

Although it would be possible to adjust the criteria for welfare and other forms of public assistance so that farmers who hold certain farming assets of value could become eligible for assistance if their incomes were low enough, the difficulty would be in the development of a politically acceptable plan with comparable eligibility criteria for both farmers and nonfarmers. The public might be willing to allow a farmer to retain some of his land or machinery and still receive benefits under a public income assistance program, but the same might not be true for urban residents. The concept of a farmer who has a net worth of $200,000, mostly in farmland, but receives public assistance payments to supplement a low, perhaps even negative, income might be politically palatable. But the concept of an urban dweller who owns a $200,000 house and receives a similar payment would probably not be politically acceptable. Costs of such a plan are also of concern if there are to be new recipients of assistance, both farm and nonfarm.

## Payment Limitation Strategies

The annual payment limitation of $50,000 per person in the existing legislation has been the only method of limiting payments to farmers and ensuring that payments are made to the farmers most in need. However, this is a crude approach. One possible difficulty is that there are farmers who would otherwise be eligible for a payment of more than $50,000, but with the $50,000 limitation and current costs and farm commodity prices, these farmers may still have only a very low, or negative net income for covering family living expenses. The basic problem remains that the criteria for income assistance under existing farm programs and under public welfare programs are very nearly opposite each other and that this ultimately leads to a long list of problems and equity considerations.

A more precise targeting of farm program benefits to low-income farmers might be accomplished within the context of new farm program legislation. Such a targeting could ultimately lead to lower federal costs for farm programs (a desirable outcome given federal budget deficits), but there are difficulties with the political realities of trying to do this—these include political problems.

The coalition that is reponsible for the basic ideas that go into farm program legislation includes players whose interests are not necessarily in keeping with revised farm legislation that would target benefits to those most in need. These players include, first of all, the commodity groups whose interest is primarily in keeping the price for their particular commodity as high as possible, not in writing legislation solely or even primarily to benefit low-income farmers. These commodity groups see low-income, small farmers as benefiting from high commodity prices, but it is the large, often high-income farmers with the most to sell who reap the greatest benefits. The second group includes the farm organization leadership, which represents primarily the commercial farmers. The leadership quite often consists of well-to-do commercial farmers who are primarily interested in extracting the maximum payment benefits for themselves. Third are the agribusiness interests, which are primarily interested in ensuring that commercial farmers have the needed dollars to purchase new tractors, fertilizer, chemicals, and so on. Agribusiness is interested in improving the incomes of low-income farmers only to the extent that this might present some limited potential for increased input sales. Fourth are the agricultural research and extension interests of the land grant system, which have, in the past, had the greatest successes in working with, directing problem-oriented research toward, and making recommendations to a comparatively well-off group of commercial farmers, not low-income farmers who lack the capital and credit sources to adopt technologies and other recommendations developed at the publicly supported land grant universities. The fifth group of players includes the large numbers of commercial farmers themselves when they start sensing that the new farm legislation is simply a public assistance program for low-income farmers with less assistance going to many of the large, efficient, and profitable farmers who are traditionally regarded as the important ones in providing consumers with abundant, low-cost food.

## Merging Farm Programs and Public Assistance

Another option is to merge existing public assistance and the current farm program payments into a comprehensive new program designed specifically to replace both the current mixture of public assistance programs and farm programs. Tax dollars now spent for farm programs and tax dollars for welfare, food stamps, and other programs to increase peoples' incomes would instead be used to fund a negative income tax program similar to that which was implemented on an experimental basis early in the 1970s. Those who report under a certain income level would receive a negative income tax payment from the federal government, which would presumably increase as the number of family members increased, but would gradually taper off as earned income increased. Appropriate scales could be developed so that it was always to the individual's benefit to earn an additional dollar, rather than receive it from the negative income tax. The value of the assets owned by the recipient would not necessarily affect eligibility, although it would be necessary to construct the legislation in such a way to ensure, for example, that individuals such as those who earn $50,000 in interest income from nontaxable state and local bonds would be ineligible.

A form of negative income tax could restore equity in income enhancement programs in the farm and nonfarm sectors. The issue of equity in income enhancement between farmers and others who receive government assistance is going to become increasingly important. It is not clear how long the current income support system which singles out farmers as a group for special and more generous treatment, can survive. There might be renewed interest in a plan similar to the negative income tax.

Such a plan would mean that prices for agricultural commodities would fall to world market levels, and supply would meet equilibrium market clearing conditions worldwide at the going world price level. Farms that could not survive would go bankrupt, and their assets would be transferred to farms that could produce at a profit given world price levels. True, some commodities might be largely produced cheaper outside the United States. There would be additional downward revaluation of farmland and other assets in agriculture, and, in the short run, federal money would be needed to assist the Farm Credit System as well as the Federal Deposit Insurance Corporation for commercial bankers in rural areas that would otherwise go under. But in a few years farmland would be valued more nearly at a level consistent with equilibrium prices, making it easier for young farmers to begin farming.

Funding for the negative income tax would come from the combination of funds now used for welfare and government farm programs. Negative income tax schedules could be developed consistent with the available revenue obtained when the current farm program and welfare legislation expires.

A major problem in constructing a feasible plan incorporating the negative income tax concept is in getting the farm-state senators and representatives with their constituency and agenda in support of farmers working together with the urban senators and representatives who have a quite different constituency and agenda in support of programs for low-income urban residents. In the past, farm-state and urban politicians have usually cooperated only to the extent deemed necessary in order to get the legislation of interest to the different constituencies passed, but not to the extent of developing comprehensive legislation that would simultaneously address the problems of both rural and urban dwellers. The political forces acting on politicians to keep farm programs and income assistance programs for urban dwellers are substantial.

## CONCLUSION

There are substantial economic and political pressures for rethinking public policies for dealing with poverty in rural areas. Overshadowing all new policy initiatives is the cost of federally administered farm programs and the magnitude of the current federal budget deficit. Given the current deficit, the federal government cannot long justify income support payments for individuals not truly in need, either to farmers or nonfarmers.

Another force is the rapid growth in government farm program payments, rising from approximately $4 billion in the 1970s to over $26 billion in the 1980s. The past rate of growth in farm program expenditures cannot long be sustained. Increased public awareness of the high current cost of government farm programs will almost assuredly lead to increased public scrutiny with respect to whether these expenditures are truly directed toward alleviating hardship in the farm sector or merely further increasing the incomes of farmers who are already doing well.

Modifications could be made in existing welfare programs in order to make the social service safety net more readily available to the rural poor who live on farms. Any change in current regulations is likely, however, to be the subject of considerable debate. This is particularly true of changes that would make asset tests less important in terms of eligibility for payments.

It is not likely that the federal government would consider funding a program structured along the negative income tax, particularly given the size of the current federal budget deficit. There is much that is still unknown about how individuals would behave with respect to work effort if a negative income tax program were in place.

Nor is it likely that the federal government will abandon efforts to assist commercial farmers through government farm programs and instead make a significant effort directed specifically at the traditional rural farm and nonfarm poor. Unlike their urban-poor counterparts, congressmen from rural districts tend to support farm programs that provide the greatest assistance to the larger commercial farmers who may be heavily in debt, or face other financial difficulties.

Strategies for industrial development are largely in control of state and local, not federal, decision makers. Rural development has the potential of being a long-term solution to poverty problems within a rural area. However, there are many rural communities that, because of locational and other disadvantages, will perhaps never be able to attract new industry. Furthermore, there is no foolproof, clear-cut strategy which a local community might pursue that would have a high probability of success. Industrial location decisions often depend on factors largely outside the control of local community leaders.

Efforts at upgrading educational and job skill levels also have the potential for providing long-term solutions to the rural poverty problem. The difficulty with these solutions is that they are long- rather than short-term programs. A state or local community may make considerable investments in educational and job skill programs, only to see participating individuals leave the community and perhaps the state once the education and job skills are attained. Despite the gains to the individual, the rural community may be no better off than before. Moreover, even with emphasis on education and job skills, it may be necessary to direct companion programs toward supporting the incomes of the rural poor in the short run, until the needed skills are obtained.

## REFERENCES

Bender, Lloyd D., et al. (1985). *The Diverse Social and Economic Structure of Nonmetropolitan America*. Economic Research Rural Development Service Reseasrch Report no. 49. U.S. Department of Agriculture. Washington, D.C.: U.S. Government Printing Office.

Cochrane, Willard. 1986. "Rural Poverty: The Failure of National Farm Programs to Deal with the Problem." *Policy Studies Journal* 15(2): 273-78.

Drabenstott, Mark. 1986. "The Long Road Back for U.S. Agriculture." *Economic Review,* The Federal Reserve Bank of Kansas City, 40-53.

Jones, Bruce L., and William D. Heffernan. 1987. "Educational and Social Programs as Responses to Farm Financial Stress." *Agricultural Finance Review* (Special issue on financial stress in agriculture) 47: 148-55.

Pasour, E. C., Jr. 1986. "Inconsistencies in U.S. Farm Policies: Implications for Change." *Forum for Applied Research and Public Policy* 2: 57-68.

Reimund, Donn, and Mindy Petrulis. 1987. "Performance of the Agricultural Sector." In *Rural Development in the 1980s: Preparing for the Future*. Agriculture and Rural Economy Division, Economic Research Service, Report no. AGES870724. U.S. Department of Agriculture. Washington, D.C.: U.S. Government Printing Office.

Rodgers, Harrell R., Jr., and Gregory R. Weiher. 1986. "The Rural Poor in America: A Statistical Overview." *Policy Studies Journal* 15(2): 279-89.

Smith, Eldon D., Brady Deaton, and David Kelch. 1978. "Locational Determinants of Manufacturing Industry in Rural Areas." *Southern Journal of Agricultural Economics* 10: 23-32.

Stone, Kenneth E. 1987. "Impact of the Farm Financial Crisis on the Retail and

Service Sectors of Rural Communities." *Agricultural Finance Review* (Special issue on financial stress in agriculture) 47: 40-47.

U.S. Department of Agriculture. 1987. "Who Gets Those Farm Program Payments?" *Farmline* (December-January): 3-9.

# 6

## Can Income Transfers Promote Economic Development in Poor, Rural Communities?

### ROBERT D. PLOTNICK

Transfer payments redistribute purchasing power among individuals. They may be made in cash, as with unemployment insurance (UI) and Aid to Families with Dependent Children (AFDC). They may be noncash, as with food stamps and Medicare. Social insurance transfers—including unemployment insurance; Social Security payments for retirement, disability, or death of a spouse; Medicare; and workers' compensation—require the recipient to have had previous earnings in order to qualify for benefits. The income-tested (or welfare) transfers, such as AFDC, Medicaid, and food stamps, are available only to persons with low incomes.

Public transfers have become a major source of personal income in the United States. In 1984, for example, they equaled $1,765 per capita, or 13.8 percent of personal income. In nonmetropolitan counties their level was slightly lower—$1,734 per capita—but as a share of personal income were more important—17.2 percent (Smith, Willis, and Weber 1987).

This study was supported in part by a grant from the Ford Foundation to the Northwest Policy Center of the Institute for Public Policy and Management, Graduate School of Public Affairs, University of Washington. The opinions expressed here do not necessarily reflect those of the foundation or the center.

Can transfer policies contribute to economic development and job creation in poor, rural communities?

At first glance, it would seem not. As currently conceived and administered, transfer programs operate outside the realm of job creation and economic development. They simply provide income support to those without a job or other private means of support.[1] While this function is an important public responsibility and significantly reduces poverty, it neither directly creates jobs nor enhances the labor market capabilities of its recipients. Thus, it is far from clear that transfers can be the focus of any strategy that can contribute to rural economic development and to the reduction of *pretransfer* poverty among rural residents.[2]

But first glances may be deceiving. The very magnitude of transfer payments, the purchasing power (hence possible job creation) they represent, and the likelihood that they will increase in importance suggest that they deserve explicit consideration by persons seeking to promote economic development. This chapter considers whether creatively recast transfer policies have the potential to serve multiple purposes: providing the "safety net" of income support and contributing to job creation and, consequently, reductions in pretransfer poverty and economic dependence. If so, these policies could usefully complement economic development strategies built around more conventional tools such as improving the educational and training skills of the local population, providing tax and other fiscal incentives for businesses to locate in certain areas, or establishing selective public subsidies and other support for local entrepreneurial initiatives. The combination of approaches might produce greater progress against poverty and dependence, and a greater contribution toward economic development, than any one approach acting in isolation.

In at least one regard transfer strategies could be more attractive than other approaches. States already spend large sums on AFDC and unemployment insurance. If reorientations of these programs can contribute to economic growth and self-sufficiency, they would come at low or no additional cost to state treasuries. If they succeed and recipients find work more quickly and collect benefits for shorter periods, state outlays may even fall. In contrast, some other approaches require net increases in spending or foregone taxes at either the state or local level, at least in the short run.

In addressing the question posed earlier, this chapter first examines the possible contribution of retirement transfers to rural economic development. It next considers the promise of using unemployment insurance more creatively to help jobless persons find work more quickly and develop alternative occupational opportunities. New initiatives seeking to turn welfare programs away from their traditional function of pure income support and toward vehicles for improving recipients' labor market skills and fostering self-sufficiency are receiving wide attention. The chapter also assesses these initiatives' potential for strengthening small communities' economies.[3]

Throughout the chapter, examples are drawn from the Pacific Northwest experience.[4]

There is no scarcity of ideas for how "transfer payment investment" strategies based on unemployment insurance and welfare might be used as tools of economic development.[5] Many have been implemented in small-scale experiments and field demonstrations in the United States by private nonprofit organizations or public agencies. Some have been enacted into law in a few states, Canada, or overseas. In principle they can be implemented in small rural communities as well as large urban ones.

What are scarce are thorough evaluations of the effectiveness of these strategies using treatment and control groups. The few careful evaluations which have been done usually either apply to programs implemented in large urban areas or do not discuss how impacts differed between urban and rural locations. Given these problems with the available evidence, the chapter's conclusions are properly viewed as tentative.

## RETIREMENT RELATED TRANSFERS AND
## SMALL COMMUNITY ECONOMIC DEVELOPMENT

Public retirement related transfers consist mainly of Social Security and Medicare. They also include the small railroad retirement program and federal, state, local, and military pensions. They provide a significant share of the purchasing power of elderly citizens. Unlike income from work, income from these sources is not tied to living in a specific community. Retirees are free to relocate anywhere in the country (or abroad) without affecting their benefits. Nonmetropolitan areas have often been the preferred destinations of retirees leaving the urban centers where they worked.[6]

Retirees bring the purchasing power of these benefits to the communities where they settle. Of roughly equal importance is the purchasing power of their private investment and pension incomes. And retirees are not disproportionately poor. Indeed, in recent years the poverty rate among persons over age sixty-five has been below the national average. Since this purchasing power stems from income generated largely outside the local community, retirees can provide the equivalent of a basic industry for some small communities.

Small communities which can attract retirees will experience increased demand for local products and services and, consequently, job growth. Since the elderly tend to purchase more heavily from local sources if the desired products and services are available, local job creation will tend to be larger than that produced by other basic industries. Local multiplier effects will magnify the initial job impact. Tighter local labor markets, in turn, will reduce poverty.

Retirement transfers are less sensitive than earnings to fluctuations in economic activity (Smith 1986). Thus, jobs generated by retirement transfers are less vulnerable to business cycles and can improve a community's capacity to adjust to changing economic conditions. In the Pacific Northwest, for example, small communities dependent on lumber, aluminum, or agriculture have been badly hurt by cyclical fluctuations and global economic restructuring. For these and many other rural communities, greater economic stability would be a welcome added benefit, beyond the new jobs, from attracting retirees.

Along with their incomes, retirees often bring significant financial assets to their new communities. Such assets can serve as a source of capital for local business enterprises.

Pursuing retirees is, then, an attractive alternative to chasing smokestacks or microchips as a way to develop or expand a small community's economic base. Small communities located near excellent recreational opportunities with mild climates are best positioned to pursue a retiree-oriented development strategy. In the Northwest, communities in coastal areas, along Puget Sound, and on the eastern slope of the Cascades in central Oregon and Washington fall into this category. Indeed, many of them currently have a relatively high proportion of elderly people or have experienced above average growth of their elderly populations.

## CAN UNEMPLOYMENT INSURANCE CONTRIBUTE TO SMALL COMMUNITY ECONOMIC DEVELOPMENT?

The existing Unemployment Insurance (UI) program provides workers with partial replacement of earnings during short periods of involuntary unemployment. A basic premise of UI is that unemployment is mainly a transitory experience caused by cyclical fluctuations in demand. Hence, workers are presumed to need only temporary income support until they are recalled by their employer or find new jobs. Typically, benefits are available for twenty-six weeks and equal 50 percent of the recipient's average weekly earnings. While receiving this support workers must actively look for jobs or risk denial of benefits.

In recent years this basic premise and, consequently, its implications for the design of UI have been increasingly challenged. In both large and small communities, structural declines in employment in manufacturing and other industrial sectors have focused attention on the problems of displaced workers—persons with substantial experience and specific skills in an industry who are on layoff and unlikely to be recalled to jobs with their old employers or in their old industry. Their prospects are dim for finding new jobs using the same skills, especially if they are reluctant to relocate.

Available published data do not provide metropolitan and nonmetropolitan area comparisons of the extent of the displaced worker problem. But there are reasons to believe it is more serious in small communities and rural areas. The economic base of a small community often depends on one major firm or industry. In the Northwest, forest products, agriculture, aluminum, and mining have served in such a role. If the local plant closes or the key industry is in decline, thee are few local alternative employment possibilities. The erosion of the economic base leads via local multiplier effects to further job losses. Extensive unemployment may persist for years. In large urban areas, in contrast, labor markets are not as thin, and the economic base is usually less closely tied to the fortunes of one firm or one industry. Laid-off workers can more easily be absorbed by other firms and industries.

Many observers are asking whether income support from UI, while the first line of defense against short-run income losses, is the best way to assist displaced workers make the long-run adjustments needed to again become productive workers.[7] New, alternative approaches to this problem have been proposed and implemented. Some, such as requiring firms to give advance notification of plant closings, assisting workers to purchase plants that otherwise would close, or establishing emergency response teams to coordinate labor, management, and public sector efforts to expeditiously place laid-off workers in new jobs, do not call for innovative uses of UI. Such efforts do not conflict with the traditional role of UI. They will not be discussed here.[8]

Approaches that do involve innovative uses of UI funds include providing enhanced job search assistance, classroom training, on-the-job training, relocation allowances, reemployment bonuses for workers who quickly find new jobs, and self-employment programs in which UI supports workers in the start-up phase of their own businesses.[9] UI recipients are relieved of the usual job search requirements in return for participating in these alternative activities. These activities do not conflict with those noted above and, indeed, might usefully complement them.

Can these UI-based innovations contribute to small community job creation, economic development, and poverty reduction?

On a conceptual level it is difficult to see how just using UI to provide classroom and on-the-job training can be relied on to create many *new* jobs, even if training can speed placement into existing jobs. To the extent that training subsidized by UI lowers firms' costs of investing in their workers, there may be a stimulus to increase employment. Such effects are likely to be modest.

There is something of a chicken-and-egg problem here, especially for small rural communities. Given the thin labor markets in small, relatively isolated communities, providing specific new job skills in the absence of a clearly identified demand for them may not help individuals find local employment. (In contrast, in a large urban labor market one could more confidently anticipate that persons given retraining will be able to use it somewhere, as long as they are not being trained for jobs in industries that are on the decline.) So, until firms locate in a small rural community, it is difficult to know what type of retraining to pursue with UI or other funds. But such communities need a skilled labor force to attract firms in the first place, especially firms offering more highly paid jobs.

The challenge for these communities, as many have recognized, is to integrate the retraining of workers carefully with the expansion plans of local enterprises and the industrial siting activities of local development agencies. Toward this end, use of UI to help finance retraining of displaced workers can make a positive contribution when combined with other economic development activities.

Similar concerns apply to enhanced job search assistance, reemployment bonuses, and relocation allowances. Careful evaluations of job search assistance and bonus schemes show they tend to reduce the duration of unemployment and outlays on UI by speeding up the matching rate between unemployed workers and jobs (Woodbury and Spiegelman 1987; Corson and Kerachsky 1987).[10] This reduces frictional unemployment and makes labor markets more efficient. But the capability of these programs to reduce structural and cyclical unemployment and to produce long-run increases in the number of jobs seems slight. Relocation allowances may help individuals find better employment opportunities and make longer run geographical adjustments of the labor force quicker and less painful. But clearly, by intent, they do not contribute to local job creation.

Programs that permit the unemployed to use UI benefits to start new businesses may hold more promise. Similar programs for welfare recipients have also been proposed. Their direct intent is to create new local job opportunities for UI or welfare recipients. Their participants do not need job offers from existing or new employers. Successful businesses would create additional jobs. More than any other initiative to use transfer programs as investments in human capital and job creation, these self-employment programs seek to transform the safety net into a ladder of economic opportunity. If such programs work, small towns and rural areas may be their most successful locales because these locations tend to have a stronger tradition of self-employment than large urban areas.

These programs have rarely been tried in the United States. Ohio fielded a small Entrepreneurial Training Pilot Project in 1985-1986. It has not been rigorously evaluated, and Ohio officials chose not to continue it. With a grant from the U.S. Department of Labor, the state of Washington will soon launch the first demonstration project of this approach, one that will be evaluated rigorously. Great Britain and France have implemented such programs nationally for several years. Although neither European program has been carefully evaluated, their experience provides a few lessons for similar initiatives here.

The British Enterprise Allowance Scheme, begun in 1982, is open to persons receiving unemployment benefits or the Supplementary Benefit (Britain's main income-tested program). It pays eligible entrepreneurs £40 per week (about $70 at the March 1988 exchange rates) for up to fifty-two weeks to supplement the income of their newly established businesses.

The French Chômeurs Créateurs (Unemployed Entrepreneurs) Program, begun in 1979, is similarly open to persons collecting either unemployment or welfare benefits. Instead of providing a weekly supplement, the program gives entrepreneurs a lump sum payment of up to 40,000 FF (about $7,000 at the March 1988 exchange rates). By the end of 1985, 234,000 persons had participated in the French program, 139,000 in the British.[11]

The British and French experiences suggest that transfer-based self-employment programs cannot be relied on as major sources of economic development and job creation for long-term unemployed and disadvantaged persons. The programs have turned only between 2 and 3 percent of transfer recipients into entrepreneurs, many of whose ventures fail. Survival rates of ventures opened under either program, however, are roughly the same as those for other small enterprises and can be increased through provision of business support services. Most of the firms set up under the programs depend on local market demand. This limits the chances for success of businesses in depressed small communities. And reliance on local markets means that new firms will compete with and displace existing firms in the same area instead of generating export earnings.

Participants for whom self-employment best served as a route to self-sufficiency tended to have above average education and business experience. The Ohio project showed a similar pattern. This implies that the programs may work better for displaced workers, who tend to have an adequate education and strong ties to the world of work, than for welfare recipients, many of whom have poor educations and minimal experience in the labor market.

On the positive side, one observes that even if a venture fails, the experience of operating it could increase the entrepreneur's confidence and credentials and contribute to his or her longer run labor market success. Perhaps friends or relatives will respond to an entrepreneurial role model and start successful businesses. While self-employment is hardly a panacea for all long-term unemployed and welfare recipients, it appears to be an option worth exploring in the U.S. context, with its strong entrepreneurial tradition. For small communities, efforts should stress developing products that can sell to persons outside the local area, thereby generating export earnings that build the local economic base and create new local jobs. Until we experiment with alternative methods of using unemployment and welfare transfers to promote self-employment, and thoroughly evaluate them, their long-run prospects will remain unknown.

## CAN WELFARE CONTRIBUTE TO SMALL COMMUNITY ECONOMIC DEVELOPMENT?

Income-tested or welfare programs provide income support to persons who satisfy the income test and meet categorical eligibility rules. Traditionally, welfare programs have simply provided a minimal level of income support to persons who lack private sources of income, either are ineligible for social insurance transfers or have exhausted eligibility for them, and are viewed as unable or unexpected to work.

The largest cash welfare program, AFDC, assists low-income families with a single parent and young children.[12] Supplemental Security Income (SSI) offers cash assistance to low-income elderly, blind, and permanently disabled persons. AFDC and SSI recipients automatically qualify for medical assistance from Medicaid, the most costly income-tested program. In some states a cash general assistance program aids needy persons who do not qualify for AFDC or SSI on categorical grounds but can meet other eligibility criteria. The food stamp program is the only welfare benefit available to all low-income Americans regardless of family structure or personal characteristics. All told there are more than seventy means-tested programs funded by federal, state, and local governments (Congressional Research Service 1987).

An earlier consensus held that AFDC is an entitlement that should simply provide income support without an expectation that recipients make sincere efforts to become self-sufficient. This consensus appears to have broken down irretrievably. The major common theme of current proposals to reform AFDC shifts the program's emphasis to a reciprocal obligation, where receiving a welfare check carries with it the expectation or, in some versions, the requirement, that a recipient look for and accept a job, or participate in education, training, or work experience activities in preparation for work. This section discusses the potential contribution of such reforms to rural economic development and antipoverty policy.[13]

The other major cash welfare programs largely assist persons widely regarded as unexpected to work. Thus, there is no interest in augmenting those programs' income support mission to add a labor market focus. This chapter will not consider how they can contribute to economic development. It also will not address income-tested noncash programs such as food stamps, housing assistance, and Medicaid. No state has proposed or implemented programs that reorient only noncash programs for job development purposes. Moreover, many recipients of such programs also receive AFDC. One may view attempts to use AFDC for job development equally well as attempts to use the larger "welfare package" of AFDC and any accompanying noncash benefits for the same purpose.

For the work/welfare reforms to succeed, there must be jobs for which welfare recipients can compete. In a recent study, L. Bloomquist, L. Jensen, and R. Teixeira (1987) [BJT] examined the labor force experience and compared the likely employment opportunities of nonmetropolitan and metropolitan welfare recipients using Current Population Survey data for 1985.

BJT found that nonmetropolitan recipients are more involved in the labor market. Over the full year 40 percent of nonmetropolitan adult AFDC recipients worked, but only 30 percent of the metropolitan ones did. Among adult recipients who did not work, 23 percent in nonmetropolitan areas but only 14 percent in metropolitan areas had looked for a job unsuccessfully. Thus, in nonmetropolitan areas, work/welfare initiatives are likely to find a more receptive clientele that is better prepared for the world of work.

To estimate the number of jobs that might be accessible to welfare clients, BJT examined the educational requirements of metropolitan and nonmetropolitan jobs and compared them to the educational levels of AFDC adults who would be expected to participate in work/welfare activities.[14] They found that 46 percent of nonmetropolitan jobs are within the ability of the work/welfare clients to perform, compared to 21 percent of metropolitan jobs.[15] This suggests that work/welfare programs have greater prospects for success in nonmetropolitan areas.

Of course, most of these jobs will already be filled and unavailable to AFDC recipients. BJT therefore estimated the likely vacancy rate in these jobs and compared the resulting number of vacant jobs to the estimated number of persons who will be expected to participate in work/welfare activities. The ratios are 3.5 work/welfare client job seekers for every nonmetropolitan job and 6.3 job seekers for every metropolitan job. While the client to available job ratio is high in both areas, conditions are more favorable in nonmetropolitan areas.

Work/welfare clients will also be competing against other unemployed persons for these jobs. When the unemployed who are not on AFDC and do not have a high school diploma (the likely competitors) are added to the estimated number of clients, the ratios jump to 9 in nonmetropolitan areas and 14 in metropolitan areas. These figures suggest it will be difficult to place welfare recipients in available jobs but again show that conditions are better in nonmetropolitan areas.

In a final analysis, BJT examined job growth trends. They showed that the kinds of jobs for which welfare recipients can qualify have grown in nonmetropolitan areas since 1980, but have declined elsewhere. Thus, like their other findings, this one implies that the situation in nonmetropolitan America is more favorable for work/welfare programs.

The BJT analysis assessed the prospects for work/welfare programs in nonmetropolitan versus metropolitan areas, but not whether such programs have, in fact, succeeded. For insight on this important question, consider the work of the Manpower Demonstration Research Corporation (MDRC). MDRC has rigorously evaluated eight work/welfare programs implemented in recent years by the states. Two of these operated largely in rural areas.

One rural program increased quarterly employment rates by 3 percent, which translated into earnings gains of 8 percent over the four quarters of follow-up experience (Gueron 1987).[16] The second had no effect on employment or earnings. This program, however, operated in West Virginia, a state with perennially high unemployment and with the nation's highest unemployment rate during part of the period studied. Partly because of the poor economic conditions, the program stressed work obligations by welfare recipients and did not offer training or job search assistance for placement in private sector jobs. In such an economic environment this type of program could reinforce community values about the importance of work, keep job skills from deteriorating, and provide useful public services, but it was unlikely to lead to gains in unsubsidized employment.

One may tentatively conclude from the MDRC research that work/welfare programs can succeed in rural areas if the local economy is not badly depressed. But, as for similar UI initiatives, job search assistance and classroom and on-the-job training cannot be relied on to create many new jobs for AFDC recipients, even if such efforts speed placement into existing jobs. To the extent that training provided by work/welfare programs lowers firms' overall labor costs, there may be a small stimulus to increase employment.

When joblessness is high, however, improving welfare recipients' job skills and helping them seek work are futile efforts, at least in the short run. If conditions improve, they may have a longer run payoff if recipients are better equipped to take advantage of emerging opportunities. Similarly, the bolder transfer payment investment strategies, which envision using welfare benefits (usually along with other sources of seed capital) to help recipients start their own businesses, face especially difficult obstacles in depressed areas.[17]

There are two important qualifications to the optimistic portion of these conclusions. First, while employment and earnings increase and dependence on welfare declines in most work/welfare programs, the changes are not dramatic. The programs as currently operated are not a panacea for poverty and economic dependence and cannot be expected to make major contributions to rural and small communities' economic health.

Second, the programs evaluated by the MDRC tended to be of short duration and limited intensity. Small returns on such small investments are to be expected. Would more costly, comprehensive programs such as Washington's Family Independence Program or Massachusetts' Employment and Training Choices have correspondingly greater success? Optimistically, one might expect bigger investments in recipients' human capital to yield bigger absolute returns.[18] But these more elaborate efforts may encounter diminishing returns and prove to be less cost effective. Only experience and continued careful evaluation will tell.

## CONCLUSION

Can transfer policies contribute to economic development, job creation and, hence, reductions in pretransfer poverty in small rural communities? Sometimes yes, sometimes no.

Attracting retirees can unquestionably generate local jobs and add an element of stability to the economic base. Realistically, this option is best pursued by communities favored by climate and location. At the same time, communities not so blessed can take steps to make themselves more appealing to their own elderly citizens. Doing so may encourage fewer elderly to leave the area, taking their assets and purchasing power with them and weakening the local economy.

Unlike retirement transfers, the states exert significant control over their UI and AFDC programs. As a result they are freer to experiment with new uses of these transfers, especially in the current climate of federal encouragement for policy innovation by the states. Of the strategies oriented around unemployment insurance, those aimed at expanding self-employment and entrepreneurial activity are the most intriguing. Small-scale experiments subject to careful evaluation are certainly in order. Available evidence from the European and Ohio experiences cautions us against having high expectations. These initiatives should probably be viewed as minor, very partial factors in job creation and antipoverty efforts. Many of the other UI strategies seem more geared to helping recipients find jobs more quickly or enhancing their job skills rather than to creating new jobs.

Like several of the UI strategies, the new work/welfare strategies tend to have more of a supply side orientation. They will help low-income persons better compete for available jobs but, by themselves, do little to expand the number of jobs. Without a healthy local economy, they are likely to be largely ineffective.

For small communities, both UI and welfare based approaches to building work skills have greater promise if they are carefully integrated with expansion plans of local enterprises and industrial siting activities of local development agencies. In communities where a strategy of attracting retirees makes sense, helping welfare clients and dislocated workers develop job skills for local businesses that serve the elderly, or helping them build new ones that serve the elderly and provide self-employment, is a possible way to combine transfer based development policies.

Any conclusions must be tentative given the meager amount of careful evidence and the lack of attention in existing evaluations to differences in program impacts between large and small, or urban and rural communities. We need much more information about what sorts of transfer based development strategies work well in which types of communities before a well-informed vision for their use can emerge.

**NOTES**

1. There have been exceptions to this general practice, of course. The Trade Adjustment Act has provided training to some unemployed workers. Although the Work Incentive Program was intended to provide training and job placement assis-

tance to large numbers of AFDC clients, funding and administrative restraints have confined services to a small proportion of them. Such efforts have always been minor appendages to the income support mission of unemployment and welfare programs.

2. Pretransfer poverty is measured by counting families' private sources of income (i.e., excluding public transfers) and comparing the results to the poverty line. For discussion of pretransfer poverty and the effect of transfers on reducing it, see Danziger, Haveman, and Plotnick (1986).

3. The chapter does not examine three other major cash transfer programs: workers' compensation, Supplemental Security Income, and veterans' pensions. Workers' compensation benefits go to persons who are not working because of short-term injuries, but who generally return to their current employers. The other two assist persons who are aged or suffer from long-term disabilities or blindness. Hence there is little interest or promise in incorporating any of these programs into labor market and economic development strategies.

4. Farm subsidy payments are conventionally classified as payments to producers, not as transfers. Consequently, this chapter does not address their role in rural economic development.

5. The Corporation for Enterprise Development (CfED) coined this phrase. CfED has actively promoted this and related strategies for economic development. See Corporation for Enterprise Development (1987a, 1987b) for a discussion of the general approach, many examples of actual programs that embody it, and a discussion of implementation strategies.

6. The material in this section is based largely on Summers and Hirschl (1985) and Smith, Willis, and Weber (1987).

7. For data and analysis on displaced workers, see Flaim and Sehgal (1985) and Podgursky and Swaim (1987).

8. For a thorough discussion of these as well as the initiatives that do involve UI, see Leigh (forthcoming).

9. For some of these initiatives, funds must be diverted from the UI system into separate accounts to satisfy legal constraints on uses of UI funds. In practical terms one can regard these as attempts to reorient UI.

10. Woodbury and Spiegelman (1987) find that workers given a $500 bonus for finding a job within eleven weeks of filing for UI benefits had spells of unemployment that averaged 1.15 weeks less than workers in the control group, who received regular UI benefits. The study does not report whether there were differences between urban and rural areas. Corson and Kerachsky's (1987) preliminary findings from the New Jersey UI Demonstration Project show similar effects of another bonus plan that was coupled with intensive job search assistance. The New Jersey project also shows that job search assistance alone, or coupled with training and relocation aid, reduces the number of weeks of UI paid relative to a control group. As one of the most urbanized states, New Jersey's experience may have little applicability to rural labor markets.

11. For program descriptions and an optimistic assessment of their potential, see Corporation for Enterprise Development (1984, 1987a). For a more pessimistic view, see Bendick and Egan (1987).

12. Some states provide AFDC to two-parent families if the second parent is unemployed, but over 90 percent of the benefits go to single-parent families.

13. Programs to promote self-employment of welfare recipients have also been proposed. Since they were discussed with the UI material, they will not be treated here.

14. BJT excluded AFDC recipients who would typically be exempted from such activities. These include single parents with children under three years of age, those already working full-time but earning so little that they qualify for some assistance, the disabled, persons over age sixty-five, and persons attending school (since they are already trying to improve their employability).

15. BJT noted several reasons why both estimates would tend to be too high. However, the ratio between them is probably roughly accurate.

16. This program operated in Virginia in seven rural and four urban agencies. Differences between rural and urban clients were not reported.

17. Actually, these conclusions would apply to any depressed area, rural or urban.

18. The experience of the Supported Work Program for long-term welfare recipients is encouraging in this regard (Hollister, Kemper, and Maynard, 1984). This experimental program provided persons with severe employment problems with work experience of about one year, under conditions of gradually increasing demands, close supervision, and peer group support. Compared to a control group, participants had significantly higher employment and earnings. Whether the program's achievements differed significantly between the urban and rural sites where it operated was not reported.

## REFERENCES

Bendick, M., and M. L. Egan. 1987. "Transfer Payment Diversion for Small Business Development: British and French Experience." *Industrial and Labor Relations Review* 37: 528-42.

Bloomquist, Leonard E., Leif Jensen, and Ray A. Teixeira. 1987. " 'Workfare' and Nonmetropolitan America: An Assessment of the Employment Opportunities for Nonmetro Welfare Clients." Paper presented at the Ninth Annual Research Conference of the Association for Public Policy Analysis and Management, Bethesda, Maryland, October 29-31.

Congressional Research Service. 1987. "Cash and Non-cash Benefits for Persons with Limited Income: Eligibility Rules, Recipient and Expenditure Data, FY 1984-86." Washington, D.C.

Corporation for Enterprise Development. 1984. "Eight Lessons from Europe." Washington, D.C.

_____. 1987a. "A Hand-up, Not a Handout: An Introduction to Transfer Investment Policy and Practice." Washington, D.C.

_____. 1987b. "How to Turn a Handout into a Hand-up: Strategies for Implementing Transfer Payment Investment." Washington, D.C.

Corson, W., and S. Kerachsky. 1987. "A Test of Early Intervention Strategies for Displaced Workers: The New Jersey Demonstration." Mathematica Policy Research. Paper presented at the Ninth Annual Research Conference of the Association for Public Policy Analysis and Management, Bethesda, Maryland, October 29-31.

Danziger, S., R. Haveman, and R. Plotnick. 1986. "Antipoverty Policy: Effects on the Poor and the Nonpoor." In *Fighting Poverty: What Works and What*

*Doesn't,* edited by S. Danziger and D. Weinberg. Cambridge, Mass.: Harvard University Press, pp. 50-72.

Flaim, P., and E. Sehgal. 1985. "Displaced Workers of 1979-1983: How Have They Fared?" *Monthly Labor Review* 108: 3-16.

Gueron, J. 1987. "State Welfare Employment Programs: Lessons from the 1980s." Paper presented at the December 1987 American Economic Association meeting.

Hollister, R., P. Kemper, and R. Maynard. 1984. *The National Supported Work Demonstration.* Madison: University of Wisconsin Press.

Leigh, D. (forthcoming). *Assisting Displaced Workers: Do the States Have a Better Idea?* Kalamazoo, Mich.: Upjohn Institute.

Mangum, S., and J. Transky. 1987. "Self-Employment Training as an Intervention Strategy for Displaced or Disadvantaged Workers." Paper presented at the December 1987 Industrial Relations Research Association meeting.

Podgursky, M., and P. Swaim. 1987. "Job Displacement and Earnings Losses: Evidence from the Displaced Worker Survey." *Industrial and Labor Relations Review* 38: 17-29.

Smith, G. 1986. "Transfer Payments and Investment Incomes: Sources of Growth and Cyclical Stability for Nonmetro Counties of Oregon and Washington." Agriculture Research Center, research bulletin 0981. Pullman: Washington State University.

Smith, G., D. Willis, and B. Weber. 1987. "The Aging Population, Retirement Income, and the Local Economy." Western Rural Development Center paper 36. Corvallis: Oregon State University.

Summers, G., and T. Hirschl. 1985. "Capturing Cash Transfer Payments and Community Economic Development." *Journal of the Community Development Society* 16: 121-32.

Woodbury, S., and R. Spiegelman. 1987. "Bonuses to Workers and Employers to Reduce Unemployment: Randomized Trials in Illinois." *American Economic Review* 77: 513-30.

# 7

# Rural Economic Development Policies for the Midwestern States

## STANLEY R. JOHNSON, DANIEL OTTO, HELEN JENSEN, and SHEILA A. MARTIN

## INTRODUCTION

The rural economy in the midwestern United States has been in economic transition since the settlement of the countryside. In the recent past, this transition has been led by a changing agriculture. The introduction of more capital-intensive agricultural technologies and the increase in farm size have caused a secular outward migration of labor from agriculture. These changes have engendered a special type of rural poverty: one where formerly prosperous regions and residents face displacement and greatly reduced standards of living. As a result, the rural economy, which has depended on agriculture, has also changed. These patterns of change and the associated economic adjustment problems have received increased public attention. The farm financial crisis of the early 1980s, the high government costs of the 1981 and 1985 farm bills, and the disparity between economic growth in the rural and nonrural economies have all combined to suggest to state and other governmental bodies the need for more coherent and realistic rural development policies.

The widespread recognition that agriculture cannot provide an economic base sufficient to sustain population and income levels consistent with those achieved in the nonagricultural sectors of the economy makes the rural development policy problem for the midwestern states especially difficult in the current era. If rural communities continue to depend on agriculture as the primary economic base, changes in economic structure are likely to be major. Population levels will continue to decline. Towns and cities depending on servicing the agricultural population for their economic welfare will adjust (Buttel 1983). And, in many cases, these adjustments will be of significant magnitude to render the associated communities nonviable as economic units.

Not surprisingly, state and local governments have initiated a myriad of policies designed to reverse these trends in population and per capita income. Unfortunately, many of these policies have been shortsighted in nature, seeking only short-term solutions to more fundamental problems. Longer term and more systematic approaches to economic policy for the rural Midwest, which are required if these policies are to do more than buffer the structural adjustment and downsizing of an economy still dependent on agriculture, are difficult to initiate. This is due in part to the relatively poorly developed economic framework on which such policies rest.

There is no agreed upon framework for achieving development in rural communities in the Midwest (Nelson 1984). It is clear that far-reaching policies, directed at structural change, will involve significant adjustment costs, borne unevenly by the current citizens of the communities. Appropriate compensation schemes will have to be integrated into these broad policy initiatives if they are to be successful. Special interest groups, representing those damaged by the policy changes, have the capability to sabotage such broad policy initiatives and, unless there are economic incentives to behave differently, they will utilize their capabilities. Accordingly, development packages must reflect the interests of those to be helped as well as those who will be injured.

This chapter can be viewed as one more step in the search for a coherent set of ideas that can be used as a basis for comprehensive rural development policies. It directs attention to evaluating what a comprehensive framework is as well as what it is not, particularly relative to past development policy initiatives. An important theme in the argument for a more realistic structure to support comprehensive development efforts is the initiation of programs to produce adequate information systems for policy design, monitoring policy change, and evaluation. Without the aid of a well-defined prescriptive framework for development, it is extremely important to have mechanisms for feedback to policymakers, enabling them to steer through what is essentially a poorly charted economic course.

## AGRICULTURE AND RURAL ECONOMIES

The difficult economic situation of the rural areas in the Midwest is easily demonstrated. The objective in this section is not to document fully the decline in the economies for midwestern communities, but instead, to show more narrowly why agriculture cannot be relied upon as the primary economic engine to drive the development process in the future. While agriculture will always be important, increased population levels and increased per capita incomes in the rural areas in midwestern states cannot be sustained on the basis of agriculture alone. Those involved in rural communities in the Midwest are aware of these difficulties. The value of this discussion will not be the enumeration of these problems but rather the documentation of the fallacy in the approaches that suggest a rekindling of economic activity and growth based on agriculture.

Figure 7.1 shows the long-term annual gulf port prices of agricultural commodities that are of primary importance in the Midwest: soybeans, corn, and wheat. Included in the figure as well are projections to the period 1995-1996. These projections incorporate "consensus" macroeconomic conditions in the United States and the rest of the world, and a continuation of current agricultural policies by the United States and major trading countries (Food and Agricultural Policy Research Institute 1988). A stark conclusion to be reached on the basis of these long-term trends in real prices is that, unless there are massive productivity increases, gross income to agriculture in the Midwest is likely to be constant or fall in real terms. Even with a highly subsidized agriculture, the Midwest can look forward to an agricultural economic base income that is at best constant in real terms. As the Food and Agricultural Policy Research Institute (FAPRI) report indicates, the secular downward decline is likely to continue, making it likely that gross receipts to agriculture will decrease rather than increase in real terms in the future.

The consequences of the change in agricultural production technology, and associated labor-saving changes in agribusiness or agriculturally supported industries, are demonstrated in Table 7.1. Table 7.1 shows nonfarm employment for the midwestern states and the United States for the period from 1960 to 1987. The trend is clear. From 1960 to 1970, the percent change in nonfarm employment was positive but in only one case equal to the national average. Some states showed employment increases greater than the national average in the 1970 to 1980 period: Kansas, Minnesota, Nebraska, and South Dakota. This situation completely reversed itself in the period from 1980 to 1984. Only Minnesota achieved the national average of a 6-percent change. Iowa and Illinois had declines of 3 and 4 percent, respectively. Finally, during the period from 1984 to 1987, employment change in the Midwest is, in some cases, at or near the national average. There is reason to be cautious about these figures, however. During this time, massive subsidies (for example, $25 billion or about 15 percent of farm gross receipts in 1986) were provided by direct government payments. Furthermore, many of the states showing strong increases in nonfarm employment achieved these increases in nonrural areas. Generally, the rural area employment decreased. Rural areas also suffer from higher levels of

**Figure 7.1**
**U.S. Gulf Port Prices**

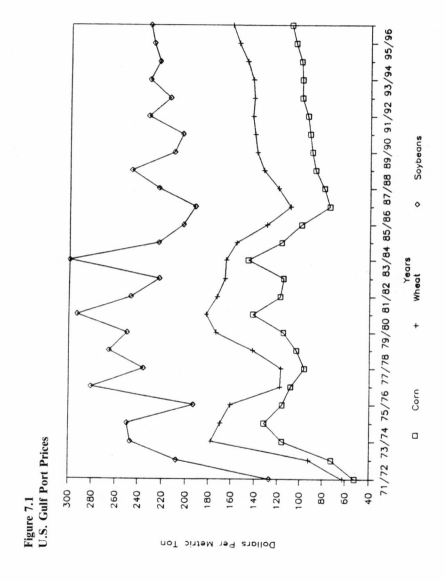

**Table 7.1**
**Total Nonfarm Employment for Midwestern States and the United States, 1960-1987**
**(in thousands)**

| | 1960 | 1970 | % Change 1960-1970 | 1980 | % Change 1970-1980 | 1984 | % Change 1980-1984 | 1987 | % Change 1984-1987 |
|---|---|---|---|---|---|---|---|---|---|
| U.S. | 52,989 | 70,644 | 33 | 90,564 | 28 | 95,882 | 6 | 102,105 | 6 |
| Iowa | 680 | 881 | 30 | 1,110 | 26 | 1,080 | (3) | 1,129 | 5 |
| Illinois | 3,417 | 4,337 | 27 | 4,892 | 13 | 4,697 | (4) | 4,934 | 5 |
| Indiana | 1,429 | 1,847 | 29 | 2,137 | 16 | 2,178 | 2 | 2,362 | 8 |
| Kansas | 557 | 677 | 22 | 949 | 40 | 977 | 3 | 1,019 | 4 |
| Minnesota | 926 | 1,309 | 41 | 1,770 | 35 | 1,883 | 6 | 1,997 | 6 |
| Missouri | 1,349 | 1,654 | 23 | 1,969 | 19 | 2,044 | 4 | 2,190 | 7 |
| Nebraska | 380 | 481 | 27 | 631 | 31 | 644 | 2 | 679 | 5 |
| South Dakota | 139 | 176 | 27 | 237 | 35 | 247 | 4 | 258 | 4 |
| Wisconsin | 1,186 | 1,535 | 29 | 1,945 | 27 | 1,990 | 2 | 2,102 | 6 |

Source: U.S. Department of Labor, Handbook of Labor Statistics, 1985.
U.S. Employment and Earnings, various issues.
Numbers in parentheses ( ) indicate negative values.

underemployment than metropolitan areas. The current data collection procedures, which focus on unemployment, mask the low pay, reduced hours, and other job limitations confronting much of the rural work force (Lichter 1987).

The personal income figures for the midwestern states compared to the United States for the period from 1960 to 1986 are shown in Table 7.2. These income figures essentially mirror the nonfarm employment figures. Although some progress is shown relative to the nation or various states, most of the personal income change has not occurred in agriculture. Behind these numbers lies the uneasy fact that gross agricultural income during the latter period has been subsidized at rates that are not likely to be sustained in the future (FAPRI 1988). In many cases the aggregate total personal income for each state shows several patterns occurring in rural areas. In rural areas with a declining employment base, wage and salary income is a declining relative share of the total personal income for the region. In rural counties where elderly and retired persons constitute a large percentage of the total population, government transfer payments and dividends, interest, and rents are becoming the major source of personal income. As a result, rural areas that have not been able to diversify and replace farm-related jobs with nonfarm employment are likely to experience increased incidences of poverty as they fall behind the growth levels of other regions.

Table 7.3 shows the net farm income (NFI) for the midwestern states from 1960 to 1986 in millions of dollars. Note that the income levels are in nominal terms; real income for agriculture has dropped precipitously over the period from 1960 to 1986. Figure 7.2 shows real farm income for the United States for the period from 1970 to 1986 with projections to 1996. This should be compared to Table 7.3, lest overly optimistic conclusions be drawn about the percent changes in nominal income. It is also important to note that the erratic nature of the change in net farm income over time is markedly affected by government payments and policies not related to agriculture.

Finally, Table 7.4 shows percent growth in employment in agriculturally related industries in the Midwest. This table indicates that the labor-saving technology that has changed the capital-labor ratio and farm size for production agriculture has also pervaded the agriculturally related industries. With some exceptions, there have been significant declines in employment. The exceptions are in agricultural services, which are not large in terms of total employment compared to the other industries. Thus, income from agriculture will be constant at best, abstracting from unanticipated technological changes. Employment multipliers on this income for agriculturally related industries are smaller now than in the past. As shown at the bottom of Table 7.4, nonagricultural manufacturing employment in the Midwest is down as well. This trend is consistent with national economic conditions. The major sources of growth for the Midwest are in government, services,

**Table 7.2**
**Total Personal Income for Midwestern States and the United States, 1960-1986**
**(in millions of dollars)**

| | 1960 | 1970 | % Change 1960-1970 | 1980 | % Change 1970-1980 | 1983 | % Change 1980-1983 | 1986 | % Change 1984-1986 |
|---|---|---|---|---|---|---|---|---|---|
| U.S. | $398,843 | $803,922 | 102 | $2,160,034 | 169 | $3,175,250 | 47 | $3,529,744 | 11 |
| Iowa | 5,539 | 10,725 | 94 | 26,829 | 150 | 37,240 | 39 | 39,296 | 6 |
| Illinois | 26,620 | 50,232 | 89 | 119,474 | 138 | 165,635 | 39 | 187,749 | 13 |
| Indiana | 10,136 | 19,433 | 92 | 49,235 | 153 | 66,929 | 36 | 75,492 | 13 |
| Kansas | 4,640 | 8,490 | 83 | 23,199 | 173 | 33,335 | 44 | 37,498 | 12 |
| Minnesota | 7,168 | 14,838 | 107 | 39,445 | 166 | 51,976 | 32 | 65,955 | 27 |
| Missouri | 9,096 | 17,360 | 91 | 43,603 | 151 | 63,587 | 46 | 72,740 | 14 |
| Nebraska | 2,845 | 5,587 | 96 | 13,968 | 150 | 22,084 | 58 | 23,043 | 4 |
| South Dakota | 1,246 | 2,093 | 68 | 5,390 | 158 | 8,096 | 50 | 8,757 | 8 |
| Wisconsin | 8,684 | 16,703 | 92 | 44,262 | 165 | 61,645 | 39 | 69,490 | 13 |

Source: U.S. Commerce Department, BEA, Local Area Personal Income.

# Table 7.3

## Net Farm Income for Midwestern States and the United States, 1960-1986
### (in millions of dollars)

| | U.S. | Iowa | Illinois | Indiana | Kansas | Minnesota | Missouri | Nebraska | South Dakota | Wisconsin |
|---|---|---|---|---|---|---|---|---|---|---|
| 1959 | $10,713 | $590 | $534 | $291 | $341 | $348 | $394 | $296 | $110 | $417 |
| 1960 | 11,211 | 611 | 534 | 347 | 396 | 448 | 381 | 328 | 272 | 371 |
| 1961 | 11,957 | 702 | 673 | 432 | 405 | 470 | 422 | 252 | 207 | 439 |
| Average NFI 1959-1961 | 11,294 | 634 | 580 | 357 | 381 | 422 | 399 | 292 | 196 | 409 |
| 1969 | 14,293 | 1,114 | 816 | 537 | 398 | 659 | 381 | 531 | 309 | 574 |
| 1970 | 14,366 | 1,080 | 630 | 363 | 538 | 816 | 447 | 468 | 328 | 576 |
| 1971 | 15,012 | 864 | 793 | 590 | 637 | 732 | 486 | 614 | 361 | 636 |
| Average NFI 1969-1971 | 14,557 | 1,019 | 746 | 497 | 524 | 736 | 438 | 538 | 333 | 595 |
| % Change 1960-1970 | 29 | 61 | 29 | 39 | 38 | 74 | 10 | 84 | 69 | 46 |
| 1979 | 31,078 | 1,846 | 1,996 | 801 | 1,140 | 1,431 | 1,261 | 1,093 | 643 | 1,530 |
| 1980 | 20,180 | 710 | 494 | 394 | 223 | 1,001 | 334 | 330 | 663 | 1,382 |
| 1981 | 29,842 | 2,096 | 1,837 | 442 | 679 | 1,266 | 894 | 1,191 | 230 | 1,327 |
| Average NFI 1979-1981 | 27,033 | 1,551 | 1,442 | 546 | 681 | 1,233 | 830 | 871 | 512 | 1,413 |
| % Change 1970-1980 | 86 | 52 | 93 | 10 | 30 | 68 | 89 | 62 | 54 | 137 |
| 1983 | 12,691 | -205 | -213 | -175 | -32 | -83 | -116 | 94 | -46 | -65 |
| 1984 | 32,022 | 1,281 | 1,182 | 763 | 812 | 1,207 | 472 | 1,184 | 551 | 1,118 |
| 1985 | 32,334 | 1,590 | 1,538 | 633 | 1,148 | 1,245 | 765 | 1,461 | 607 | 1,049 |
| 1986 | 37,484 | 2,331 | 1,475 | 705 | 1,477 | 1,670 | 698 | 1,773 | 754 | 1,562 |
| Average NFI 1984-1986 | 28,633 | 1,249 | 996 | 482 | 851 | 1,010 | 455 | 1,128 | 467 | 916 |
| % Change 1980-1986 | 6 | (19) | (31) | (12) | 25 | (18) | (45) | 29 | (9) | (35) |

Source: U.S.D.A., Economic Indicators of the Farm Sector, U.S.D.A., Farm Income Data: A Historical Perspective, 1986.
Numbers in parentheses ( ) indicate negative values.

**Figure 7.2**
**U.S. Net Farm Income and Government Payments**

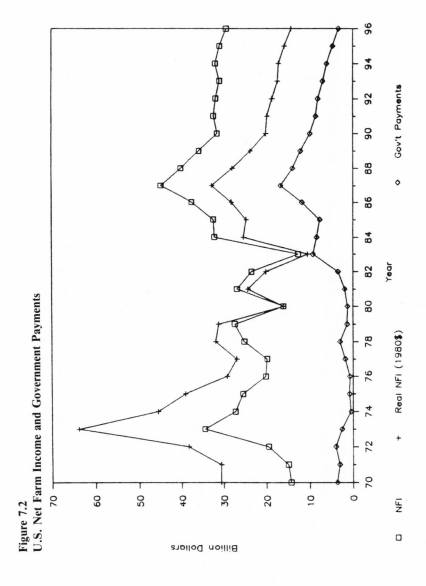

**Table 7.4**

**Employment and Percentage of Growth in Employment in Agriculturally Related Industries in the Midwest, 1970-1980 and 1980-1985**

|                              | U.S.       | Iowa    | Illinois  | Indiana |
|------------------------------|------------|---------|-----------|---------|
| **Agricultural Services**    |            |         |           |         |
| 1970                         | 189,026    | 3,449   | 5,831     | 2,917   |
| 1980                         | 315,200    | 3,642   | 8,299     | 4,068   |
| 1985                         | 519,700    | 3,992   | 11,814    | 6,224   |
| % Change 1970-1980           | 67         | 6       | 42        | 39      |
| % Change 1980-1985           | 65         | 10      | 42        | 53      |
| **Food Products**            |            |         |           |         |
| 1970                         | 1,595,472  | 49,949  | 118,787   | 40,337  |
| 1980                         | 2,384,700  | 46,035  | 95,610    | 35,884  |
| 1985                         | 2,884,300  | 38,355  | 82,639    | 33,442  |
| % Change 1970-1980           | 49         | (8)     | (20)      | (11)    |
| % Change 1980-1985           | 21         | (17)    | (14)      | (7)     |
| **Lumber & Wood Prod.**      |            |         |           |         |
| 1970                         | 554,835    | 3,678   | 12,000    | 11,495  |
| 1980                         | 897,100    | 5,034   | 12,263    | 19,310  |
| 1985                         | 1,127,800  | 4,408   | 10,770    | 17,914  |
| % Change 1970-1980           | 62         | 37      | 2         | 68      |
| % Change 1980-1985           | 26         | (12)    | (12)      | (7)     |
| **Agricultural Chemicals**   |            |         |           |         |
| 1970                         | 51,095     | 1,203   | 1,635     | 1,566   |
| 1980                         | 107,200    | 1,381   | 1,926     | 1,806   |
| 1985                         | 123,600    | 1,569   | 726       | 1,819   |
| % Change 1970-1980           | 110        | 15      | 18        | 15      |
| % Change 1980-1985           | 15         | 14      | (62)      | 1       |
| **Farm Machinery**           |            |         |           |         |
| 1970                         | 126,958    | 21,173  | 28,835    | 5,942   |
| 1980                         | 298,400    | 29,039  | 22,914    | 5,748   |
| 1985                         | 207,100    | 14,296  | 11,829    | 2,854   |
| % Change 1970-1980           | 135        | 37      | (21)      | (3)     |
| % Change 1980-1985           | (31)       | (51)    | (48)      | (50)    |
| **Non-Ag Manufacturing**     |            |         |           |         |
| 1970                         | 16,947,840 | 138,026 | 1,206,214 | 654,108 |
| 1980                         | 31,991,900 | 176,455 | 1,167,311 | 621,836 |
| 1985                         | 41,437,300 | 142,788 | 936,787   | 550,368 |
| % Change 1970-1980           | 89         | 28      | (3)       | (5)     |
| % Change 1980-1985           | 30         | (19)    | (20)      | (11)    |

Source: U.S. Department of Commerce, County Business Patterns. "D" denotes figures withheld to avoid disclosure of operations of individual establishments. Numbers in parentheses ( ) indicate negative values.

Table 7.4 (continued)

| Kansas | Minnesota | Missouri | Nebraska | South Dakota | Wisconsin |
|--------|-----------|----------|----------|--------------|-----------|
| 2,546 | 2,757 | 3,543 | 1,754 | (D) | 3,287 |
| 2,210 | 3,778 | 4,888 | 1,954 | 606 | 43,017 |
| 3,140 | 4,555 | 6,086 | 6,498 | 954 | 5,777 |
| (13) | 37 | 38 | 11 | (D) | 1,209 |
| 42 | 21 | 25 | 233 | 57 | (87) |
| | | | | | |
| 18,024 | 45,481 | 44,920 | 24,930 | 7,134 | 53,848 |
| 22,773 | 39,861 | 39,940 | 24,768 | 7,743 | 54,300 |
| 24,658 | 37,614 | 36,421 | 23,229 | 7,387 | 50,023 |
| 26 | (12) | (11) | (1) | 9 | 1 |
| 8 | (6) | (9) | (6) | (5) | (8) |
| | | | | | |
| (D) | 7,514 | 7,907 | (D) | 679 | 15,814 |
| 3,704 | 13,699 | 10,486 | 2,378 | 1,583 | 21,910 |
| 3,144 | 12,748 | 8,657 | 1,777 | 1,457 | 19,757 |
| (D) | 82 | 33 | (D) | 133 | 39 |
| (15) | (7) | (17) | (25) | (8) | (10) |
| | | | | | |
| (D) | 411 | 743 | 220 | (D) | (D) |
| (D) | 478 | 3,328 | 693 | (D) | 394 |
| 506 | 311 | 2,744 | 827 | 26 | 458 |
| (D) | 16 | 348 | 215 | (D) | (D) |
| (D) | (35) | (18) | 19 | (D) | 16 |
| | | | | | |
| 4,495 | 5,046 | 2,648 | 4,176 | 325 | 14,168 |
| 8,319 | 7,124 | (D) | 9,085 | 1,561 | 18,133 |
| 4,966 | 3,357 | 1,278 | 5,596 | 520 | 9,801 |
| 85 | 41 | (D) | 118 | 380 | 28 |
| (40) | (53) | (D) | (38) | (67) | (46) |
| | | | | | |
| 119,510 | 266,900 | 402,388 | 56,958 | 7,709 | 432,430 |
| 172,406 | 331,580 | 404,606 | 63,912 | 16,374 | 476,647 |
| 152,465 | 331,546 | 376,995 | 60,482 | 17,736 | 417,794 |
| 44 | 24 | 1 | 12 | 112 | 10 |
| (12) | (0) | (7) | (5) | 8 | (12) |

finance, and industries in the nonmanufacturing sectors (Bureau of Labor Statistics).

Thus, as stated at the beginning of this section, the evidence shows that agricultural income is unlikely to grow. Changing technologies for agriculture suggest that if income remains constant, employment in agriculture will decrease. Employment multipliers for agricultural income in the agriculturally related industries are becoming smaller, as these industries reorganize and utilize labor-saving technologies. Nonagricultural manufacturing employment is decreasing in the Midwest more rapidly than nationally. These broad trends give some evidence as to where economic development policies might be directed. Reversing the trend of the Midwest compared to the rest of the United States for nonmanufacturing is a possibility. Concentration on forms of employment in rapid-growth industries, which are not locationally tied, seems an appropriate general direction for development policy.

## DEVELOPMENT POLICY OBJECTIVES

The most commonly articulated economic development policy objectives involve income and employment. In fact, comparisons of economic status among communities, states, and nations frequently involve per capita income. Increased employment is important in this context since it is indicative of the total income. However, these comparisons fail to go beyond these generally accepted indices of development to investigate the development perceptions of the citizens, particularly in rural communities. More precise identification of development perceptions of affected populations can provide the basis for an improved framework for development policy. In a sense, these more specific objectives provide guidelines as to how it will be politically acceptable to organize and stimulate the changes that will lead to improved per capita income and higher employment.

As a result of an admitted relatively unsystematic review of the rhetoric on economic development for rural communities in the Midwest, four of these more refined perceptions of development objectives emerge: restoration, distribution, a biological model, and underperformance. Many of the development initiatives and articulated development goals of midwestern states can be classified as designed to achieve these more specific objectives. All, of course, are appropriate and achievable in certain circumstances. The question for the rural communities in the Midwest and for the development policy framework is whether these objectives are attainable given the underlying trends in agriculture and agriculturally related industries.

### Restoration

Those who would reverse the modern technology-driven changes in the structure of agriculture and revitalize the rural communities to return to a condition existing at some time in the distant past are arguing for development policies that stress economic restoration. The Harkin-Gephardt Bill, introduced during the 1985 Farm Bill debate, is an example of a policy approach directed toward achieving higher income and increased employment through restoration of agriculture and rural communities. Generally, these policies have the disadvantage of involving large dead-weight welfare losses, which are associated with the economic distortions that the policies would indicate. Although substantial income could be moved back into the rural communities, this movement of income would come at a substantial cost to society. Perhaps a more lucid example of restoration as a development policy objective is a valley that experiences disastrous floods. Here, the idea of restoring the communities in the valley to a previous state is relatively easy to articulate, and the policies to achieve these results are easily determined as well.

Two points are in order. First, policies aimed at restoration of the economic structure and activity in rural communities must be directed at the agricultural sector. Communities in the past were based on a different type of agriculture and were fostered by policies appropriate to that previous era. Second, success for the restoration ideas might require going beyond agriculture to the agriculturally related industries, where the consequences of technical change for employment and income have paralleled those in agriculture. Our general conclusion is that restoration, although an appropriate objective in some isolated and special development contexts, is losing ground as a guiding principle or objective for rural economic development in the midwestern states.

### Distribution

A second concept of development refers to distribution or inequities in the economic system. These types of concerns with economic development have led to targeted assistance programs. Examples of these programs include those directed to the poor in the U.S. economy: food stamps, Aid to Families with Dependent Children, disaster assistance, educational loans, and others. An interesting feature of all of these distributional policies is an implicit assumption that they are short term in duration. In the short run, affected households or individuals are being assisted on a temporary basis, until they can participate more fully in the economic growth or the economy in the region. In the Midwest, these distributional problems are important and could provide a basis for the development of compensation types of policies. If the economies change, compensation may be due those who are affected negatively in order to benefit society as a whole. As the economy is currently evolving, there are problems of distribution. The smaller agricultural base implies a downsizing of the agricultural service industries and other adjustments. Perhaps a political basis for development policy will have to include elements of distribution that can provide the basis for a compensation scheme.

## A Biological Model

A third development perception can be described as biological in nature. Here, the development process is seen as something similar to the process occurring in an ecosystem. Niches evolve that permit "economic opportunities." Rural communities, and more generally, the rural sector, are encouraged to take advantage of these opportunities. Policies are organized, not to change the structure of the communities, but instead to support these opportunity areas. Cottage industries, linkages between rural and urban communities to take advantage of excess labor, new product development, and identification of non–location-specific industries are examples of the kinds of ideas that dominate these perceptions of objectives for economic growth. This is a very passive type of economic growth objective. It appears to have been embraced by many of the public support services. This is, perhaps, an unrealistic approach to growth, if the major economic base of the communities is declining, as in the Midwest. Still, there are advantages to seeing growth objectives in terms of the biological framework. Policies related to increased employment and per capita income through the biological approach can be easily identified. A major question for this ecosystem view of economics is whether the system can be sustained at its current energy level without the infusion of a source of income and employment to counter the declines in agriculture.

## Underperformance

An emerging concept of development objectives involves the idea of economic underperformance. The economic underperformance objectives involve comparisons. These comparisons can be to other rural communities, other states, or other nations. Essentially, the idea is to compare employment growth and employment patterns as well as per capita income to that in other areas. Two possibilities exist under this framework. In the first case, the population can move to other areas, adjusting the employment levels and per capita incomes so that they are more comparable. Alternatively, policy initiatives can be undertaken to maintain or increase current population and employment levels and corresponding per capita incomes. This approach guides policymakers to the primary sources of income and ultimately, in the case of the Midwest, to a concern about the size of dimensions of the state rural economies that can be supported by an agricultural sector as it is currently structured, or as it will be in the future. The approach also is useful in developing and transmitting examples of successful policies. Of course, the factors that account for the success of these policies need to be understood, but some general features emerge. Economic diversification, multiple primary industries, the importance of research and investment in human capital and infrastructure, and other factors emerge immediately as important if the underperformance objective is accepted.

In a recent program, conducted by Pioneer Hi-Bred International of Des Moines, Iowa, rural economic development was addressed. The program, called "Search for Solutions," was novel in origin. The idea of the program was to bring together Pioneer employees who are largely residents of rural communities in the midwestern states to discuss economic development possibilities. Common approaches to economic development were sought, and employees were encouraged to become involved in these economic development efforts.

As a part of the rural economic development program of the Search for Solutions project at Pioneer, a survey was conducted (Jensen et al. 1987). This survey was made of Pioneer employees who reside in rural communities. One of the questions on this survey referred to what have been called here specialized perceptions of development objectives. The question was: "Which of the following phrases best characterizes the rural development aspirations of your community: Need to restore former economic vitality; there is uneven performance, some businesses and families are doing well and some not; and the community is not performing as well as it could with the resources available." Of those responding to the questionnaire, 22 percent elected the first option, 57 percent elected the second option, and 21 percent elected the third option. These results were relatively surprising to the conference organizers. They are believed to illustrate two things. First, these communities are in transition, and the effects of the transition are being felt unevenly by members of the rural communities. A strong basis for compensation as an integral part of development policies thus emerges. Second, there is a nearly even balance between those who would restore the communities to their former structure and economic levels and those who are more concerned with underperformance. The emerging interest in underperformance, although not well stated in this questionnaire, is of interest. The questionnaire provides evidence, albeit weak, that the underperformance and distributional concerns about economic development together dominate the restoration perception. Biological perception was not included in the questionnaire, but much of the conference involved these ideas. Such ideas are appealing because they hold out the promise of economic growth and development in the communities without fundamental structural change.

## PAST POLICY APPROACHES

Past policy approaches have implicitly or explicitly involved a type of production function concept for economic development. A number of attempts have been made to classify or provide a taxonomy for these approaches both in economic and in other areas (Edwards 1981; Warren 1963). The discussion by Edwards, which has received wide attention among agricultural economists, has been influential in fashioning rural development policies in the U.S. Department of Agriculture, state government, and local communities. This framework identifies five approaches to rural development policy: resources availability, technology, expanding markets, space and location, and institutions. The ideas implicit in the framework are summarized briefly. It is noteworthy that, at least in our characterization of the summarization, there is an absence of measures that could support the underperformance or distributional economic development objectives. Generally, the idea implicit in many of these approaches and in the Edwards scheme is to somehow reach a higher level of development with the same type of economic structure. Inequities are not addressed, and significant changes in structure are excluded, except perhaps in the ideas of institutions.

### Resource Availability

Increasing resource availability to stimulate economic development is consistent with neoclassical economic theory. According to the theory, variations in economic growth among regions are explained by differences in resource productivity and endowments. Policies suggested by this theory relate to changing resource endowments and productivity through organization, technology transfer, regulating markets, taxes and income transfers, and other means. For productivity growth, endowments remain unchanged, but output is increased through technology policy, e.g., education, infrastructure, and other public actions, increasing output and ultimately the income of the region. At the regional level, tax and transfer policies are important determinants of economic incentives and growth as well.

### Technology

Technology is widely acknowledged as an important ingredient in economic growth and development policy. However, when it comes to defining processes for generating new technology and diffusion or technology adoption, the inadequacies of the current theory become apparent. The theory of technology and economic growth includes a set of not fully integrated hypotheses on new technologies, diffusion, and adoption. All of these add to aggregate cohesiveness necessary for communities to adapt over time (Warren 1963). Other examples of using technology as a growth strategy are increasing productivity, increasing efficiency, changing structure, and creating new products or new uses for existing outputs. It is clear from the history of economic growth that technology has played an important role in improving economic status. Exactly how the technology is developed, diffused, and adopted is more problematic.

## Expanding Markets

Many of the abrupt changes in economic growth historically have been related to market patterns and expansion. This has occurred particularly for communities specializing in agricultural commodities traded internationally. Expanding markets drive up prices, resulting in increased investment in human and physical capital and increased output. Returns to factors of production are increased, as is income. How markets are expanded and how the expansion is stimulated are matters less well understood. We know what to do if the markets expand but not how the market expansions occur.

## Space and Location

Space or location theory is highly developed and has a strong and integrated theoretical foundation. A central element of this study is the introduction of space, in addition to time, in models of economic activity and growth. The theory and applied results emphasize the importance of location patterns, agglomeration, transportation, and other spatial dimensions of economic activity. Policies to improve economic development and growth derived from location theory relate to proximity of natural resources, linkages among industries or firms, regional specialization, and, more generally, the implications of acknowledging the importance of spatial patterns in regionalization and economic growth.

## Institutions

Institutions are widely recognized as important in facilitating economic growth and development. Theories of institution building emphasize infrastructure as a contributor to economic growth. How societies invest in infrastructure and what motivates this investment activity represent important areas for economic growth research. Generally, since many services are public goods, private industry, if left alone to supply them, will underinvest simply because the economic benefits of the expanded services are not appropriable. Thus, much of the work and theory relating institutions to growth are concerned with public services. This approach to economic development has been most eclectic and multidisciplinary.

These development ideas of Edwards and Warren are heavily rooted in agriculture as the primary engine driving the economies of rural communities, implicitly or explicitly. They have merit in guiding policies that will increase the efficiency of these communities and enable them to capitalize on agriculture more fully as the primary industry. They do not deal with the problem of the probable declining gross income for agriculture in midwestern rural communities and the subsequent necessity for adapting mechanisms of structural change of the economies. They also fail to address compensation for losers in the adjustment processes. These points do not invalidate these approaches, but they indicate that there may be additional steps or additional concepts necessary to provide a framework that can allow policymakers in rural communities and midwestern states to formulate development alternatives that can be politically acceptable and at the same time achieve significant economic progress.

## A RURAL ECONOMIC DEVELOPMENT POLICY FRAMEWORK

The trends that have been documented for agriculture and for agriculturally related industries in the Midwest, relating to farm size and estimates of the cost of significant policies to transfer income to the agricultural sector (FAPRI 1987; FAPRI 1988), suggest that the biological and restoration perceptions of development objectives are not viable. Of course, there are special circumstances in which these approaches are viable for rural communities. These have been indicated to an extent in the discussion of the perceptions. However, as principles to govern general development strategies, both are lacking.

The more plausible possibilities for erecting politically acceptable and sustainable economic development policies are distribution and underperformance. Distribution raises the whole idea of compensation to buffer adjustment costs and facilitate acceptance of development policies that imply significant changes in economic structure. Underperformance casts the development problem in relative terms and is more appropriate for high-income societies. As important, the underperformance perception argues for far more efficient, timely, and comprehensive information systems to support the development process. Economic units to which comparisons are being made must be fully understood, and the circumstances in the target regions for economic policy must be identified. Finally, development policies must be carefully monitored. Clearly, although the general objectives are improvement in employment and per capita income, the framework for development is limited to a loose comparison. This implies that increased observation and feedback to policymakers are necessary to ensure that development policies are achieving desired objectives or are at least moving toward those objectives.

The rural development policy framework advocated involves five steps:

• Develop systematic comparisons with other economies or economic units.

• Select growth targets and objectives.

• Organize the processes to achieve these growth targets, including appropriate changes in institutions.

• Carefully monitor and evaluate policy impacts.

• Recognize economic development policy as essentially a high-tech science.

A few comments about the approach are provided below. Obviously, the approach is exploratory at this point, but it is advanced as a method for pushing beyond the methods provided by the current, largely ineffective approaches to rural economic development policy.

### Develop Systematic Comparisons

Since there is not a widely agreed upon framework for development in rural communities, examples or role models for rural communities may be the most important source of information on development strategies. These comparisons must be made in a systematic manner. Anecdotal evidence is not useful. Frequently, there are factors not included in review of anecdotal incidence that are responsible for the changes. Longer term performance should be evaluated, and careful information should be obtained about the development policy successes. This information should include not only the industry or base industry in question but also the political structure, the taxing and income mechanisms, and any other factors that identify the full environment within which industries operate. As emphasized, the call is for significant investment in intelligence about development processes and successful development programs.

### Select Growth Strategies

A general growth strategy for states and regions should be identified. This permits coordinated administration of economic development policies. In the past, the midwestern states have advocated development programs on a more ad hoc basis. The result is a myriad of policies frequently working at cross-purposes with each other. A comparison of a state's approaches to those taken by modern large corporations would provide a basis for evaluation of decision-making processes. Successful corporations take full advantage of high-technology information and intelligence. No corporation enters a new market or a new era without careful evaluation. Specific targets are set. Those responsible for the process are evaluated relative to the achievement of these targets. The development program or package is implemented very systematically. Growth strategies, targets, and packaging of approaches are essential features to the achievement of success in developing rural communities.

### Organize to Achieve the Objectives

Many of the obstacles to development and growth of rural communities involve inequitable distributions of resources. The implications of these inequities from changes in economic structures must be addressed directly. Appropriate compensation schemes must be developed. It must be clear to the population in general that the communities or states will be better off as a whole, including the compensation, than before. There is nothing morally wrong with compensation. In fact, what is being achieved is a change in economic structure. Economic factors that forfeit rents associated with past structures must be compensated in order to make the policy changes viable.

There are additional questions with respect to the "appropriate" levels of private and public infrastructure. Communities often have high taxes because they are operating public services at uneconomic scales. Generally, it is apparent that there are size thresholds for communities to operate various services efficiently. These must be recognized, and appropriate changes must be made through cooperation, contracting with other communities, or even relocation of the sites or individuals (perhaps involving compensation). All this implies very extensive development of information systems, so that those affected can be sure about the outcomes, whether they are related to compensation or to the transfer mechanisms that would facilitate the appropriate compensations to achieve the objectives.

### Monitor and Evaluate

As mentioned several times previously, a general framework for development does not exist. Under such circumstances, careful and timely management must be substituted for broadly accepted principles. But careful and timely management requires information. Essentially, the emphasis in economic development is on the management of change, however selected, more than on the identification of a particular paradigm that leads all participants who somehow agree with it in the direction of improved levels of economic activity. The economic principles involved are rent seeking, second or even third best, and other types of policies for which existing economic theories provide little guidance. The idea is to integrate what we know about incentives, responses, compensation, and economic activity more generally into an effective management strategy. Public policy management will become a more important idea in the development of rural economic development policy.

### Recognize High-Tech Science

The days of philosophizing about development change for rural America in the midwestern states have passed. Very sophisticated management strategies will be required to achieve increased per capita incomes and increased employment in rural midwestern communities. Changes in the very structures of the communities will be required. Sophisticated compensation schemes will be necessary to sustain changes, and timely intervention by policymakers or those responsible for administering development programs must be achieved. In short, the process of achieving economic development policy change for rural communities and improving employment and income status will require advanced methods of processing and utilizing information. These advanced methods include better sensing and sampling, more timely processing, and developing systems that can organize and utilize the information effectively. Carefully defined development packages must be produced, and the capacity for change and adaptation based on feedback from relatively current experiences must be made. Additionally, the comparisons to other communities, states, and organizations must be continual. Economic processes do not stand still. Technology grows rapidly, and the process for economic development and economic development policy must be continuous and evolutionary.

Most, if not all, of the information and data required to implement and support this policy framework centers around state and local sources. With the federal government's withdrawal from local economic activity concerns and the decline of federally supported data systems, the states themselves must take much of the initiative. An encouraging possibility is the fact that there are many unorthodox data bases. Indicators can be developed from the data available from private industry or currently collected for state regulation agencies. Much more broad concepts for data bases, appropriate indicators, development objectives, and other factors associated with the process are prerequisites to a successful economic development policy.

The American Statistical Association has recognized the growing need for and opportunities for development of state and local statistical policies (Lehren 1988). As responsibilities for many social programs have shifted away from the federal government, state agencies have developed a need for information, but they have also begun to generate information as a by-product of administrating such programs. Coordination of efforts among state and local governments is essential for the maximization of the informational benefits of statistical collecting and reporting.

It may be feasible to use the Bureau of Economic Analysis (BEA) system of leading, lagging, and coincident indicators as a model from which to formulate local economic indicators. Gerhard Bry and Charlotte Boschan (1971) encourage local use of BEA-type indicators by pointing out that their development and analysis would enable policymakers not only to compare performance across regions, but also to evaluate past development efforts and to use these evaluations as feedback to the policy-making process. To a limited degree, this BEA system has been used as a model for the development of a set of indicators for the state of New Jersey to monitor business cycle expansion and contraction (Loeb 1975). A completely developed system would require taking into account many of the same factors used by the BEA to determine the usefulness of an indicator. These factors include economic significance, statistical adequacy, timing, conformity, and currency (Zarnowitz and Boschan 1975).

## SUMMARY AND CONCLUSIONS

This chapter has examined the recent economic development experiences and needs of the rural Midwest and has reviewed the traditional policy approaches prescribed for dealing with rural area problems. Without a generally accepted framework to guide economic development policy, a myriad of initiatives have been proposed to deal with declining population and income trends in rural areas. This chapter has proposed a somewhat different approach to economic development policy for the midwestern states. In part, the arguments have grown from frustration with past development policies in which states have failed to recognize the underlying changes in economic structure that have led to the current depressed conditions. Also, economic development policy has been seen more as an art than as a science.

The process for developing rural economic policies must be brought to a more scientific basis if it is to be both sustainable and politically sound. The framework advocated here is one which takes advantage of modern developments in information processing and management systems.

Information systems must be more timely, development approaches must be more targeted, processes must be carefully monitored as they evolve, and efficient systems for managing the information and disseminating it must be developed. All of this information is costly, but the evolving information policy suggests that such a system is achievable.

## REFERENCES

Bry, Gerhard, and Charlotte Boschan. 1971. *Cyclical Analysis of Time Series: Selected Procedures and Computer Programs.* New York: National Bureau of Economics Research.

Bureau of Labor Statistics. 1985. "Employment of Wage and Salary Workers by Industry, 1984, and Projected 1995 Alternatives." Washington, D.C.: U.S. Department of Labor.

Buttel, Frederick H. 1983. "Farm Structure and the Quality of Life in Agricultural Communities: A Review of Literature and a Look toward the Future." In

*Agricultural Communities: The Interrelationship of Agriculture, Business, Industry, and Government in the Rural Economy.* Congressional Research Service, Committee on Agriculture, U.S. House of Representatives.

Edwards, Clark. 1981. "The Bases for Regional Growth: A Review." *A Survey of Economic Literature.* Vol. 3, Lee R. Martin, ed. Minneapolis: University of Minnesota Press.

———. 1976. "The Political Economy of Rural Development: Theoretical Perspectives." *American Journal of Agricultural Economics* 58: 914-22.

Food and Agricultural Policy Research Institute. 1988. "FAPRI Ten-Year International Agricultural Outlook." Staff Report 1-88. Ames: Center for Agricultural and Rural Development, Iowa State University.

Jensen, H. H., S. R. Johnson, S. A. Martin, and D. M. Otto. 1987. "Report on Data from Participants." Report presented at the Pioneer Hi-Bred International Search for Solutions in Economic Development II Conference, Des Moines, Iowa. Ames: Center for Agricultural and Rural Development.

Lehren, Robert G. 1988. "Statistical Policy for State and Local Governments." *The American Statistician* 42(1): 10-16.

Lichter, Daniel T. 1987. "Measuring Underemployment in Rural Areas." *Rural Development Perspectives* 4(2): 11-14.

Loeb, P. 1983. "Leading and Coincident Indicators of Recession and Recovery in New Jersey." In *Essays in Regional Economic Studies,* edited by Dutta et al. Durham, N.C.: Acorn Press.

Nelson, Glenn L. 1984. "Elements of a Paradigm for Rural Development." *American Journal of Agricultural Economics* 66:694-701.

U.S. Department of Agriculture. *Economic Indicators of the Farm Sector.* Assorted issues.

U.S. Department of Agriculture, Economic Research Service. 1986. *Farm Income Data: A Historical Perspective.* Statistical Bulletin 740.

U.S. Department of Commerce. *County Business Patterns.* Assorted issues.

U.S. Department of Commerce, Bureau of Economic Analysis. *Local Area Personal Income.* Assorted issues.

Warren, Roland L. 1963. *The Community in America.* Chicago: Rand McNally.

Zarnowitz, Victor, and Charlotte Boschan. May 1975. "Cyclical Indicators and Evaluation and New Leading Indicators." *Business Conditions Digest* 12(5): v-xix.

# Bibliography

Albrecht, D. E., and S. H. Murdock. 1987. *The Farm Crisis in Texas: Changes in the Financial Condition of Texas Farmers and Ranchers, 1985-86.* TAES Technical Report no. 87-3. College Station: Texas Agricultural Experiment Station.
_____. 1988. *The Implications of the Farm Crisis for the Residents and Businesses of Rural Communities.* TAES Technical Report no. 88-4. College Station: Texas Agricultural Experiment Station.
Albrecht, D. E., et al. 1987. *Farm Crisis: Impact on Producers and Rural Communities in Texas.* TAES Technical Report no. 87-5. College Station: Texas Agricultural Experiment Station.
Albrecht, D. E., S. H. Murdock, and R. Hamm. 1988. "The Consequences of the Farm Crisis for Rural Communities." *Journal of the Community Development Society* 19(2): 119-35.
Auletta, Ken. 1982. *The Underclass.* New York: Random House.
Avery, R. B., G. E. Elliehausen, and G. B. Canner. 1984. "Survey of Consumer Finances, 1983." *Federal Reserve Bulletin* 70: 679-92.
Barry, P. J. 1986. *Financial Stress in Agriculture: Policy and Financial Consequences.* Department of Agricultural Economics, Report no. AE4621. Champaign: University of Illinois at Urbana.
Bender, L. D., et al. 1985. *The Diverse Social and Economic Structure of Nonmetropolitan America.* Economic Research Service, Rural Development Research Report no. 9. U.S. Department of Agriculture. Washington, D.C.: U.S. Government Printing Office.

Bendick, M., and M. L. Egan. 1987. "Transfer Payment Diversion for Small Busi-
    ness Development: British and French Experience." *Industrial and Labor
    Relations Review* 37: 528-42.
Bentley, S. 1987. "Income Transfers, Taxes, and the Poor." *Rural Development
    Perspectives* 3: 30-33.
Bianchi, Suzanne M., and Daphne Spain. 1986. *American Women in Transition*. A
    Census Monograph Series. New York: Russell Sage Foundation.
Bloomquist, L. E. 1987. "Performance of the Rural Manufacturing Sectors." In
    *Rural Economic Development in the 1980s: Preparing for the Future.*
    Agriculture and Rural Economy Division, Economic Research Service,
    Report no. AGES870724. U.S. Department of Agriculture. Washington,
    D.C.: U.S. Government Printing Office.
Bloomquist, Leonard E., Leif Jensen, and Ray A. Teixeira. 1987. " 'Workfare' and
    Nonmetropolitan America: An Assessment of the Employment Opportuni-
    ties for Nonmetro Welfare Clients." Paper presented at the Ninth Annual
    Research Conference of the Association for Public Policy Analysis and Man-
    agement, Bethesda, Maryland, October 29-31.
Brown, D. L., and K. L. Deavers. 1987. "Rural Change and the Rural Economic
    Policy Agenda for the 1980s." In *Rural Economic Development in the 1980s:
    Preparing for the Future.* Agriculture and Rural Economy Division,
    Economic Research Service, Report no. AGES870724. U.S. Department of
    Agriculture. Washington, D.C.: U.S. Government Printing Office.
Bry, Gerhard, and Charlotte Boschan. 1971. *Cyclical Analysis of Time Series:
    Selected Procedures and Computer Programs.* New York: National Bureau
    of Economics Research.
Bultena, G., et al. 1986. "The Farm Crisis: Patterns and Impacts of Financial
    Distress among Iowa Farm Families." *Rural Sociology* 51(4): 436-48.
Buttel, Frederick H. 1983. "Farm Structure and the Quality of Life in Agricultural
    Communities: A Review of Literature and a Look toward the Future." In
    *Agricultural Communities: The Interrelationship of Agriculture, Business,
    Industry, and Government in the Rural Economy.* Congressional Research
    Service, Committee on Agriculture, U.S. House of Representatives.
Carlson, John E., Marie L. Lassey, and William R. Lassey. 1981. *Rural Society and
    Environment in America.* New York: McGraw-Hill.
Cochrane, Willard. 1986. "Rural Poverty: The Failure of National Farm Programs
    to Deal with the Problem." *Policy Studies Journal* 15(2): 273-78.
Congressional Research Service. 1987. "Cash and Non-cash Benefits for Persons
    with Limited Income: Eligibility Rules, Recipient and Expenditure Data, FY
    1984-86." Washington, D.C.
Corporation for Enterprise Development. 1984. "Eight Lessons from Europe."
    Washington, D.C.
————. 1987a. "A Hand-up, Not a Handout: An Introduction to Transfer Invest-
    ment Policy and Practice." Washington, D.C.
————. 1987b. "How to Turn a Handout into a Hand-up: Strategies for Imple-
    menting Transfer Payment Investment." Washington, D.C.
Corson, W., and S. Kerachsky. 1987. "A Test of Early Intervention Strategies for
    Displaced Workers: The New Jersey Demonstration." Mathematica Policy
    Research. Paper presented at the Ninth Annual Research Conference of the

Association for Public Policy Analysis and Management, Bethesda, Maryland, October 29-31.

Council of Economic Advisors. 1965. "Some Economic Tasks of the Great Society." B. A. Weisbrod, ed. *The Economics of Poverty.* Englewood Cliffs, N.J.: Prentice-Hall.

Danziger, S., R. Haveman, and R. Plotnick. 1986. "Antipoverty Policy: Effects on the Poor and the Nonpoor." In *Fighting Poverty: What Works and What Doesn't,* edited by S. Danziger and D. Weinberg. Cambridge, Mass.: Harvard University Press.

Deavers, Kenneth L., Robert A. Hoppe, and Peggy J. Ross. 1986. "Public Policy and Rural Poverty: A View from the 1980s." *Policy Studies Journal* 15(2): 291-309.

Doeksen, G. A. 1987. "The Agricultural Crisis As It Affects Rural Communities." *Journal of the Community Development Society* 18(1): 78-88.

Doeksen, G. A., and J. Peterson. 1987. *Critical Issues in the Delivery of Local Government Services in Rural America.* Agriculture and Rural Economics Division, Economic Research Service, Staff Report AGES860917. U.S. Department of Agriculture. Washington, D.C.: U.S. Government Printing Office.

Drabenstott, Mark. 1986. "The Long Road Back for U.S. Agriculture." *Economic Review,* The Rederal Reserve Bank of Kansas City, 40-53.

Dunn, J. C. 1987. "Rural Farm Population Loss: Economic and Demographic Implications for North Dakota's State Planning, Region 6." Master's thesis, North Dakota State University, Fargo.

Edwards, Clark. 1981. "The Bases for Regional Growth: A Review." *A Survey of Economic Literature.* Vol. 3, Lee R. Martin, ed. Minneapolis: University of Minnesota Press.

_____. 1976. "The Political Economy of Rural Development: Theoretical Perspectives." *American Journal of Agricultural Economics* 58: 914-22.

Engels, R. A. 1986. "The Metropolitan/Nonmetropolitan Population at Mid-Decade. Paper presented at the annual meeting of the Population Association of America, San Francisco.

Flaim, P., and E. Sehgal. 1985. "Displaced Workers of 1979-1983: How Have They Fared?" *Monthly Labor Review* 108: 3-16.

Food and Agricultural Policy Research Institute. 1988. "FAPRI Ten Year International Agricultural Outlook." Staff Report 1-88.

Fuguitt, G. V. 1985. "The Nonmetropolitan Population Turnaround." *Annual Review of Sociology* 11: 259-80.

Garfinkel, Irwin, and Sara S. McLanahan. 1985. "The Feminization of Poverty: Nature, Causes, and a Partial Cure." Discussion paper 776-85, Institute for Research on Poverty. Madison: University of Wisconsin.

_____. 1986. *Single Mothers and Their Children: A New American Dilemma.* Washington, D.C.: Urban Institute Press.

Ghelfi, Linda M. 1987. "Income, Needs and Expenditures: Metro-Nonmetro Differences in Wisconsin." Paper presented at the 50th annual meeting of the Rural Sociology Society, Madison, Wisconsin, August 13-15.

Ginder, R. G. 1985. *The Structure of Production Agriculture and the Farm Debt Crisis.* Ames: Iowa State University.

Goreham, G. A., et al. 1987. "Implications of Trade and Market Patterns of North Dakota Farm and Ranch Operators." *North Dakota Farm Research* 44(4): 23-27.

Gueron, J. 1987. "State Welfare Employment Programs: Lessons from the 1980s." Paper presented at the December 1987 American Economic Association meeting.

Habib, J., M. Kohn, and R. Lerman. 1977. "The Effect on Poverty Status in Israel of Considering Wealth and Variability of Income." *Review of Income and Wealth* 23: 17-38.

Haveman, R. H. 1988. "Facts vs. Fiction in Social Policy." *Challenge* 31: 23-28.

_____. 1987. *Poverty Policy and Policy Research: The Great Society and the Social Sciences.* Madison: University of Wisconsin Press.

Heffernan, J. B., and W. D. Heffernan. 1985. *The Effects of the Agricultural Crisis on the Health and Lives of Farm Families.* Columbia: University of Missouri.

Henry, M., et al. 1986. "A Changing Rural America." *Economic Review* 71: 23-41.

Hollister, R., P. Kemper, and R. Maynard. 1984. *The National Supported Work Demonstration.* Madison: University of Wisconsin Press.

Hopkins, Kevin R. 1987. *Welfare Dependency: Behavior, Culture, and Public Policy.* U.S. Department of Health and Human Services, OS, ASPE. Washington, D.C.: U.S. Government Printing Office.

Hoppe, Robert A. 1980. "Despite Progress, Rural Poverty Demands Attention." *Rural Development Perspectives* (March): 7-10.

Institute for Research on Poverty, University of Wisconsin, Madison. 1980. "On Not Reaching the Rural Poor: Urban Bias in Poverty Policy." *Focus* 4(2): 5-8.

Jensen, H. H., S. R. Johnson, S. A. Martin, and D. M. Otto. 1987. "Report on Data from Participants." Center for Agricultural and Rural Development. Report presented at the Pioneer Hi-Bred International Search for Solutions in Economic Development II Conference, Des Moines, Iowa.

Jensen, Leif. 1987. "Rural Minority Families in the United States: A Twenty-Year Profile of Poverty and Economic Well-Being." Paper presented at the 50th annual meeting of the Rural Sociological Society, Madison, Wisconsin, August 13-15.

Johnson, J., et al. 1987. *Financial Characteristics of U.S. Farms, January 1, 1987.* Economic Research Service, Agricultural Information Bulletin, no. 525. U.S. Department of Agriculture. Washington, D.C.: U.S. Government Printing Office.

_____. 1986. *Financial Characteristics of U.S. Farms, January 1, 1986.* Economic Research Service, Agricultural Information Bulletin no. 500. U.S. Department of Agriculture. Washington, D.C.: U.S. Government Printing Office.

_____. 1985. *Financial Characteristics of U.S. Farms, 1985.* Economic Research Service, Agricultural Information Bulletin no. 495. U.S. Department of Agriculture. Washington, D.C.: U.S. Government Printing Office.

Johnson, J. D., et al. 1984. "Financial Conditions of the Farm Sector and Farm Operators." *Agricultural Finance Review* 47: 1-18.

Johnson, K. M. 1985. *The Impact of Population Change on Business Activity in Rural America.* Boulder, Colo.: Westview Press.

Jones, Bruce L., and William D. Heffernan. 1987. "Educational and Social

Programs as Responses to Farm Financial Stress." *Agricultural Finance Review* 47: 148-55.

Kitagawa, Evelyn M. 1955. "Components of a Difference between Two Rates." *Journal of the American Statistical Association* 50: 1168-94.

Knudsen, Patrick L. 1987. "After Long, Bruising Battle, House Approves Welfare Bill." *Congressional Quarterly* (December 19): 3157-65.

Korsching, P. F., and J. Gildner, eds. 1986. *Interdependencies of Agriculture and Rural Communities in the Twenty-First Century: The North Central Region Conference Proceedings.* Ames: The North Central Regional Center for Rural Development, Iowa State University.

Leholm, A. G., et al. 1985. *Selected Financial and Other Socioeconomic Characteristics of North Dakota Farm and Ranch Operators.* Ag. Eco. Report no. 199. Fargo: North Dakota State University.

Lehren, Robert G. 1988. "Statistical Policy for State and Local Governments." *The American Statistician* 42(1): 10-16.

Leigh, D. Forthcoming. *Assisting Displaced Workers: Do the States Have a Better Idea?* Kalamazoo, Mich.: Upjohn Institute.

Lerman, D. L. 1988. "Rural Portfolios." Economic Research Service, U.S. Department of Agriculture (unpublished draft).

Lerman, D. L., and R. I. Lerman. 1986. "Income from Owner-Occupied Housing and Income Inequality." *Urban Studies* 23: 323-31.

Lerman, D. L., and J. J. Mikesell. 1988. "Impacts of Adding Net Worth to the Poverty Definition." *Eastern Economic Journal.*

Levitan, Sar. 1985. *Programs in Aid of the Poor.* 5th ed. Baltimore, Md.: The Johns Hopkins University Press.

Lichter, Daniel T. 1987. "Measuring Underemployment in Rural Areas." *Rural Development Perspectives* 4(2): 11-14.

Long, R. W., et al. 1987. *Rural Policy Formulation in the United States.* Agriculture and Rural Economics Division, Economic Research Service, Staff Report no. AGES870203. U.S. Department of Agriculture. Washington, D.C.: U.S. Government Printing Office.

Mangum, S., and J. Transky. 1987. "Self-Employment Training as an Intervention Strategy for Displaced or Disadvantaged Workers." Paper presented at the December 1987 Industrial Relations Research Association meeting.

Marousek, G. 1979. "Farm Size and Rural Communities: Some Economic Relationships." *Southern Journal of Agricultural Economics* 2(2): 61-65.

Morrissey, E. S. 1985. *Characteristics of Poverty in Nonmetro Counties.* Economic Development Division, Economic Research Service, Rural Development Research Report no. 52. U.S. Department of Agriculture. Washington, D.C.: U.S. Government Printing Office.

Murdock, S. H., and F. L. Leistritz. 1988. *The Farm Financial Crisis: Socioeconomic Dimensions and Implications for Producers and Rural Areas.* Boulder, Colo.: Westview Press.

Murdock, S. H., et al. 1985. *The Farm Crisis in Texas: An Examination of the Characteristics of Farmers and Ranchers under Financial Stress in Texas.* Department of Rural Sociology Technical Report 85-2. College Station: Texas Agricultural Experiment Station.

———. 1987. "Impacts of the Farm Crisis on a Rural Community." *Journal of the*

    *Community Development Society* 18(1): 30-49.

_____. 1988. "The Implications of the Current Farm Crisis for Rural America." In *The Farm Financial Crisis: Socioeconomic Dimensions and Implications for Producers and Rural Areas,* ed. Murdock and Leistritz. Boulder, Colo.: Westview Press.

_____. 1986. "The State of Socioeconomic Impact Analysis in the United States: Limitations and Opportunities for Alternative Futures." *Journal of Environmental Management* 23: 99-117.

Murray, Charles. 1984. *Losing Ground: American Social Policy, 1950-1980.* New York: Basic Books.

Nelson, Glenn L. 1984. "Elements of a Paradigm for Rural Development." *American Journal of Agricultural Economics* 66: 694-701.

O'Connell, Martin, and David E. Bloom. 1987. "Cutting the Apron Strings: Women in the Labor Force in the 1980s." Discussion paper 87-1, Center for Population Studies. Cambridge, Mass.: Harvard University.

O'Hare, William P. 1988. "The Rise of Poverty in Rural America." Population Trends and Public Policy, paper no. 15 (July). Washington, D.C.: Population Reference Bureau, Inc.

Oppenheimer, Valerie K. 1970. *The Female Labor Force in the United States.* Population Monograph Series, no. 5. Berkeley: University of California.

Orshansky, M. 1965. "Counting the Poor: Another Look at the Poverty Profile." *Social Security Bulletn* 28: 3-29.

Pasour, E. C., Jr. 1986. "Inconsistencies in U.S. Farm Policies: Implications for Change." *Forum for Applied Research and Public Policy* 2: 57-68.

Podgursky, M., and P. Swaim. 1987. "Job Displacement and Earnings Losses: Evidence from the Displaced Worker Survey." *Industrial and Labor Relations Review* 38: 17-29.

Popovich, M. G. 1987. *State Emergency Farm Finance.* Vol. 2. Washington, D.C.: Council of State Policy and Planning Agencies.

Rank, Mark R., and Thomas A. Hirschl. 1988. "A Rural-Urban Comparison of Welfare Exits: The Importance of Population Density." *Rural Sociology* 53(2): 190-206.

Reimund, Donn, and Mindy Petrulis. 1987. "Performance of the Agricultural Sector." In *Rural Economic Development in the 1980s: Preparing for the Future.* Agriculture and Rural Economy Division, Economic Research Service, Report no. AGES870724. U.S. Department of Agriculture. Washington, D.C.: U.S. Government Printing Office.

Richter, K. 1985. "Nonmetropolitan Growth in the Late 1970s: The End of the Turnaround?" *Demography* 22: 245-63.

Ricketts, Erol R., and Isabel V. Sawhill. 1985. "Defining and Measuring the Underclass." *Journal of Policy Analysis and Management* 7(2): 316-25.

Rodgers, Harrell R., Jr., and Gregory R. Weiher. 1986. "The Rural Poor in America: A Statistical Overview." *Policy Studies Journal* 15(2): 279-89.

Ross, Peggy J., and Elizabeth S. Morrissey. 1986. "Persistent Poverty among the Nonmetropolitan Poor." Paper given at Southern Rural Sociological Association, February 4, Orlando, Florida.

Sawhill, I. V. 1988. "Poverty in the U.S.: Why Is It So Persistent?" *Journal of Economic Literature* 26: 1073-119.

Schiller, Bradley R. 1980. *The Economics of Poverty and Discrimination.* 3d ed. Englewood Cliffs, N.J.: Prentice-Hall.

Slesinger, Doris P., and Eleanor Cautley, 1986. "Determinants of Poverty among Rural and Urban Women Who Live Alone." Working paper 86-43, Center for Demography and Ecology. Madison: University of Wisconsin.

Smith, Eldon D., Brady Deaton, and David Kelch. 1978. "Locational Determinants of Manufacturing Industry in Rural Areas." *Southern Journal of Agricultural Economics* 10: 23-32.

Smith, G. 1986. "Transfer Payments and Investment Incomes: Sources of Growth and Cyclical Stability for Nonmetro Counties of Oregon and Washington." Agriculture Research Center, research bulletin 0981. Pullman: Washington State University.

Smith, G., D. Willis, and B. Weber. 1987. "The Aging Population, Retirement Income, and the Local Economy." Western Rural Development Center paper 36, Corvallis: Oregon State University.

Stinson, J., et al. 1986. *Governing the Heartlands: Can Rural Communities Survive the Farm Crisis?* A report prepared for the Senate Subcommittee on Intergovernmental Relations. Washington, D.C.: U.S. Congress.

Stone, Kenneth E. 1987. "Impact of the Farm Financial Crisis on the Retail and Service Sectors of Rural Communities." *Agricultural Finance Review* 47: 40-47.

Summers, G., and T. Hirschl. 1985. "Capturing Cash Transfer Payments and Community Economic Development." *Journal of the Community Development Society* 16: 121-32.

Taeuber, Cynthia M., and Victor Valdisera. 1986. "Women in the American Economy." *Current Population Reports,* Special Studies Series P-23, no. 146. U.S. Bureau of the Census. Washington, D.C.: U.S. Government Printing Office.

U.S. Bureau of the Census. 1984. *Characteristics of the Poverty Population below the Poverty Level: 1982.* Current Population Reports, Series P-60, no. 144. Washington, D.C.: U.S. Government Printing Office.

———. 1987. "Money Income and Poverty Status of Families and Persons in the United States: 1986." Current Population Reports, Series P-60, no. 157. (Advance data from the March 1987 Current Population Survey.) Washington, D.C.: U.S. Government Printing Office.

———. 1983. *1980 Census of Population and Housing, General Social and Economic Characteristics, United States Summary.* Vol. 1, ch. C, PC80-1-C1. Washington, D.C.: U.S. Government Printing Office.

U.S. Department of Agriculture. 1987. "Who Gets Those Farm Program Payments?" *Farmline* (December-January): 3-9.

Waite, Linda J. 1981. "U.S. Women at Work." *Population Bulletin* 36(2). Washington, D.C.: Population Reference Bureau.

Warren, Roland L. 1963. *The Community in America.* Chicago: Rand McNally.

Watkins, Julia M., and Dennis A. Watkins. 1984. *Social Policy and the Rural Setting.* New York: Springer.

Weicher, J. C. 1987. "Mismeasuring Poverty and Progress." *Cato Journal* 6: 715-30.

Weisbrod, B. A. 1965. "The Economics of Poverty: An American Paradox." In

*The Economics of Poverty,* B. A. Weisbrod, ed. Englewood Cliffs, N.J.: Prentice-Hall.

Weisbrod, B. A., and W. L. Hansen. 1968. "An Income-Net Worth Approach to Measuring Economic Welfare." *American Economic Review* 58: 1315-29.

Wilson, William Julius. 1987. *The Truly Disadvantaged: The Inner City, the Underclass, and Public Policy.* Chicago: University of Chicago Press.

Woodbury, S., and R. Spiegelman. 1987. "Bonuses to Workers and Employers to Reduce Unemployment: Randomized Trials in Illinois." *American Economic Review* 77: 513-30.

# Index

# About the Editors and Contributors

DON E. ALBRECHT received his Ph.D. from Iowa State University in rural sociology. He is currently an associate professor in the Department of Rural Sociology at Texas A&M, specializing in research on the sociology of agriculture and the impacts of changes in agriculture structure on rural communities.

KENNETH BACKMAN is a Ph.D. candidate in urban and regional science at Texas A&M. He is currently conducting research on rural economic development and its implications for rural and service areas.

ELEANOR CAUTLEY is a master's degree candidate in the Department of Rural Sociology, University of Wisconsin-Madison. She is also a research specialist in that department and has worked on research concerning migrant agricultural workers, maternal and infant health care, and women who head households.

DAVID L. DEBERTIN received his Ph.D. from Purdue University in agricultural economics. He is currently a professor of agricultural economics at the University of Kentucky, specializing in resource and policy economics.

RITA R. HAMM received her master's degree in political science from Florida Atlantic University, Boca Raton. She is currently a research associate in the Department of Rural Sociology at Texas A&M University.

CRAIG L. INFANGER is an extension professor of agricultural economics at the University of Kentucky, specializing in agricultural and rural policy. He received his Ph.D. from Washington State University in agricultural economics.

HELEN JENSEN received her Ph.D. from the University of Wisconsin-Madison in agricultural economics. Her current title is associate professor in the Department of Economics at Iowa State University. Interests include consumption economics, food and nutrition policy.

LEIF JENSEN received his Ph.D. from the University of Wisconsin-Madison in sociology. He is currently an assistant professor of sociology at Bates College, Lewiston, Maine, with special interests in demography and social stratification.

STANLEY R. JOHNSON received his Ph.D. from Texas A&M University in agricultural economics. He is currently the administrator for the Center for Agricultural and Rural Development at Iowa State University. Special areas of interest include food and nutrition policy.

F. LARRY LEISTRITZ received his Ph.D. from the University of Nebraska in philosophy. He is currently professor of agricultural economics at North Dakota State University, Fargo. Special areas of interest include economic impact of resource development, economic determinants and consequences of farm financial crisis, resource economics, fiscal analysis, and socioeconomic impact modelling.

DONALD L. LERMAN has a Ph.D. in economics from the University of Wisconsin-Madison. An author of numerous articles in the fields of urban public finance and income inequality, he is presently an economist with the Economic Research Service, U.S. Department of Agriculture.

SHEILA A. MARTIN is a graduate student working on her master's degree in agricultural economics. She is currently a graduate research assistant in the Department of Economics at Iowa State University.

JAMES J. MIKESELL has a Ph.D. in economics from Iowa State University. Currently an economist with the Economic Research Service, U.S. Department of Agriculture, he has written numerous articles on financial, housing, education, and regional economics topics, with frequent emphasis on implications for rural economies.

STEVE H. MURDOCK received his Ph.D. from the University of Kentucky, Lexington, in sociology. He is currently professor and head of the Department of Rural Sociology at Texas A&M with special interests in demography, human ecology, socioeconomic impact analysis, community, applied sociology, rural sociology, economic development, and evaluation research.

DANIEL OTTO received his Ph.D. from Virginia Tech in agricultural economics. He is currently associate professor of economics and extension economist at Iowa State University. Special areas of interest include community and rural economic development, impact analysis, and economic feasibility analysis of public services and facilities.

ROBERT D. PLOTNICK is an associate professor of public affairs and social work at the University of Washington. His research interests include antipoverty, income support, and labor market policies and benefit-cost analysis of social service programs.

LLOYD POTTER is a Ph.D. candidate in demography at the University of Texas at Austin Population Research Center. He is currently working on the analysis of mortality and socioeconomic patterns in rural areas.

HARRELL R. RODGERS, JR., received his Ph.D. in political science from the University of Iowa. He is a professor of political science at the University of Houston. He is a policy analyst who specializes in poverty.

DORIS P. SLESINGER is currently chair and professor of rural sociology at the University of Wisconsin-Madison. She has published numerous articles on the demography and health of rural populations, including migrant agricultural workers, hispanics, blacks, and native Americans. She received her Ph.D. from the University of Wisconsin-Madison in sociology.

GREGORY WEIHER has a Ph.D. in political science from Washington University in St. Louis. He is an assistant professor in the Department of Political Science at the University of Houston. He is a policy analyst who specializes in political economics.